"Congress shall make no law . . . abridging the freedom of speech, or of the press."

First Amendment to the US Constitution

The basic foundation of our democracy is the First Amendment guarantee of freedom of expression. The Opposing Viewpoints Series is dedicated to the concept of this basic freedom and the idea that it is more important to practice it than to enshrine it.

OPPOSING VIEWPOINTS® SERIES

Medical Testing

Noël Merino, Book Editor

GREENHAVEN PRESS
A part of Gale, Cengage Learning

GALE
CENGAGE Learning·

Farmington Hills, Mich • San Francisco • New York • Waterville, Maine
Meriden, Conn • Mason, Ohio • Chicago

Elizabeth Des Chenes, *Director, Content Strategy*
Cynthia Sanner, *Publisher*
Douglas Dentino, *Manager, New Product*

For more information, contact:
Greenhaven Press
27500 Drake Rd.
Farmington Hills, MI 48331-3535
Or you can visit our Internet site at gale.cengage.com

Articles in Greenhaven Press anthologies are often edited for length to meet page requirements. In addition, original titles of these works are changed to clearly present the main thesis and to explicitly indicate the author's opinion. Every effort is made to ensure that Greenhaven Press accurately reflects the original intent of the authors. Every effort has been made to trace the owners of copyrighted material.

Cover image copyright © Darren Baker/Shutterstock.com.

LIBRARY OF CONGRESS CATALOGING-IN-PUBLICATION DATA

Medical testing / Noël Merino, book editor.
    pages cm. -- (Opposing viewpoints)
  Includes bibliographical references and index.
  ISBN 978-0-7377-6959-3 (hardback) -- ISBN 978-0-7377-6960-9 (paperback)
  1. Drugs--Testing--Juvenile literature. 2. Clinical trials--Juvenile literature. I. Merino, Noël.
    RM301.27.M43 2014
    615.1072'4--dc23

                                                            2013033389

Printed in the United States of America
  1 2 3 4 5   18 17 16 15 14

OPPOSING
VIEWPOINTS®
SERIES

Medical Testing

Other Books of Related Interest:

Opposing Viewpoints Series

Alternative Medicine

Medical Technology

At Issue Series

Animal Experimentation

The Ethics of Medical Testing

Current Controversies Series

Prescription Drugs

Contents

Chapter 3: What Are Some Concerns About Diagnostic Medical Tests?

Chapter 4: What Are Some Concerns About Genetic Testing?

Why Consider Opposing Viewpoints?

> "The only way in which a human being can make some approach to knowing the whole of a subject is by hearing what can be said about it by persons of every variety of opinion and studying all modes in which it can be looked at by every character of mind. No wise man ever acquired his wisdom in any mode but this."
>
> *John Stuart Mill*

In our media-intensive culture it is not difficult to find differing opinions. Thousands of newspapers and magazines and dozens of radio and television talk shows resound with differing points of view. The difficulty lies in deciding which opinion to agree with and which "experts" seem the most credible. The more inundated we become with differing opinions and claims, the more essential it is to hone critical reading and thinking skills to evaluate these ideas. Opposing Viewpoints books address this problem directly by presenting stimulating debates that can be used to enhance and teach these skills. The varied opinions contained in each book examine many different aspects of a single issue. While examining these conveniently edited opposing views, readers can develop critical thinking skills such as the ability to compare and contrast authors' credibility, facts, argumentation styles, use of persuasive techniques, and other stylistic tools. In short, the Opposing Viewpoints Series is an ideal way to attain the higher-level thinking and reading skills so essential in a culture of diverse and contradictory opinions.

In addition to providing a tool for critical thinking, Opposing Viewpoints books challenge readers to question their own strongly held opinions and assumptions. Most people form their opinions on the basis of upbringing, peer pressure, and personal, cultural, or professional bias. By reading carefully balanced opposing views, readers must directly confront new ideas as well as the opinions of those with whom they disagree. This is not to simplistically argue that everyone who reads opposing views will—or should—change his or her opinion. Instead, the series enhances readers' understanding of their own views by encouraging confrontation with opposing ideas. Careful examination of others' views can lead to the readers' understanding of the logical inconsistencies in their own opinions, perspective on why they hold an opinion, and the consideration of the possibility that their opinion requires further evaluation.

Evaluating Other Opinions

To ensure that this type of examination occurs, Opposing Viewpoints books present all types of opinions. Prominent spokespeople on different sides of each issue as well as well-known professionals from many disciplines challenge the reader. An additional goal of the series is to provide a forum for other, less known, or even unpopular viewpoints. The opinion of an ordinary person who has had to make the decision to cut off life support from a terminally ill relative, for example, may be just as valuable and provide just as much insight as a medical ethicist's professional opinion. The editors have two additional purposes in including these less known views. One, the editors encourage readers to respect others' opinions—even when not enhanced by professional credibility. It is only by reading or listening to and objectively evaluating others' ideas that one can determine whether they are worthy of consideration. Two, the inclusion of such viewpoints encourages the important critical thinking skill of objectively evaluating an author's credentials and bias. This evaluation will illuminate an author's reasons for taking a particular stance on an issue and will aid in readers' evaluation of the author's ideas.

It is our hope that these books will give readers a deeper understanding of the issues debated and an appreciation of the complexity of even seemingly simple issues when good and honest people disagree. This awareness is particularly important in a democratic society such as ours in which people enter into public debate to determine the common good. Those with whom one disagrees should not be regarded as enemies but rather as people whose views deserve careful examination and may shed light on one's own.

Thomas Jefferson once said that "difference of opinion leads to inquiry, and inquiry to truth." Jefferson, a broadly educated man, argued that "if a nation expects to be ignorant and free . . . it expects what never was and never will be." As individuals and as a nation, it is imperative that we consider the opinions of others and examine them with skill and discernment. The Opposing Viewpoints Series is intended to help readers achieve this goal.

David L. Bender and Bruno Leone,
Founders

Introduction

"I want to be assured that current rules for research participants protect people from harm or unethical treatment, domestically as well as internationally."

President Barack Obama,
"Presidential Memorandum:
Review of Human Subjects Protection,"
November 24, 2010

There are a variety of ways in which medical testing impacts our lives. Modern medical tests can diagnose disease, screen for early signs of disease, and monitor response to medical treatment. These types of medical tests can involve physical tests done during an examination such as a simple breathing test through spirometry; tests of blood, urine, or tissue samples to check for the presence of pathogens or hormone levels, among other indicators; radiologic tests from x-ray radiography, ultrasound, computed tomography (CT), or magnetic resonance imaging (MRI) to check for growths or broken bones; or genetic tests to check for the presence of genetic markers for disease. With increased accuracy, lower cost, and greater availability of many tests, doctors and patients have become more likely to request tests, which has prompted several concerns.

H. Gilbert Welch, a professor of medicine at the Dartmouth Institute for Health Policy and Clinical Practice and coauthor of *Overdiagnosed: Making People Sick in the Pursuit of Health*, says, "Both patients and doctors have I think in the past viewed testing as something like, 'How can you go wrong? It never hurts to know.' It's only been recently that we've sort of realized that in fact testing can unearth the start of a whole chain of events that aren't in the patient's interests." Concerns about the dangers of certain tests, the effects of unnecessary treatment for conditions that may resolve on their own, and the cost of testing have led many to criticize a policy of erring on the side of performing a test when it is not clearly warranted. Nonetheless, whether one is considering the wisdom of yearly mammograms or a cholesterol test, there is always the small number of people who will find the cancerous lump or evidence of heart disease, thus providing a justification for widespread testing.

Beyond the controversial issues surrounding medical tests used for diagnosis and screening, there is also controversy regarding the testing done on human subjects and animal subjects to study the progress of disease and determine the efficacy of various medical treatments. Before medicines and treatments are approved for use in humans, research is usually undertaken first in animals and then in humans through clinical trials. Both types of research are controversial for different reasons.

Most medical research performed on animals involves mice, rats, fish, and birds. The US Department of Agriculture estimates that of the 26 million animals used for research, testing, and educational purposes in 2010, approximately 25 million were mice, rats, fish, and birds. The remaining 1 million animals included approximately 70,000 nonhuman primates, 65,000 dogs, and 22,000 cats. Public opinion is divided on the morality of using animals for medical testing: In a 2010 Gallup poll, 59 percent of Americans endorsed medical testing on animals as morally acceptable, whereas 34 percent found it to be morally wrong. In a 2011 poll, the science journal *Nature* found that among biomedical scientists, 63.1 percent strongly agreed and 28.6 percent agreed with the statement, "Animal research is essential to the advancement of biomedical science." Five percent neither agreed nor disagreed, whereas only 2.6 percent disagreed. Clearly, scientists have yet to make their case to the general public and controversy still abounds.

Medical testing performed on human subjects research is less controversial regarding the research itself, with controversy existing primarily with respect to how the research is conducted and how the human subjects are treated during clinical trials. Clinical research can involve people who have disease and those who are healthy, but medical testing of the former is generally less controversial than the latter, although concerns still exist. The main concerns about clinical research involve issues of informed consent, risks to the participants, and vulnerable populations.

The recent uncovering of a medical testing scandal in Guatemala illustrates a situation where each of these concerns was vindicated. In 2010, the United States formally apologized to Guatemala for leading human experiments from 1946 to 1948 where Guatemalan soldiers, prostitutes, prisoners, and mental patients were purposely infected with syphilis and other sexually transmitted diseases to study the effects of antibiotics. The subjects did not give their informed consent to participate, the experiments put them at risk (at least eighty-three subjects died), and the study purposely focused on highly vulnerable populations. Although the scandal occurred several decades ago, the unearthing of it was a reminder that the concerns about human subjects research are not without merit.

Exploring a variety of controversies surrounding medical tests and medical research, the authors in *Opposing Viewpoints: Medical Testing* offer competing views in the following chapters: What Are Some Concerns Regarding the Testing of New Medicine?, How Should Medical Testing on Humans and Animals Be Regulated?, What Are Some Concerns About Diagnostic Medical Tests?, and What Are Some Concerns About Genetic Testing? The views in this anthology offer different perspectives on these topics and illustrate the importance of the issues in informing future policy.

What Are Some Concerns Regarding the Testing of New Medicine?

Chapter Preface

Concerns about the testing of new medicine have often stemmed from abuses or scandals regarding past testing. During World War II, Nazi Germany conducted medical experiments on large numbers of prisoners held in concentration camps. Many of the experiments aimed to improve medical treatment such as malaria immunization and hypothermia treatment. These experiments on prisoners, who were coerced into participating, often resulted in their death or disfigurement. During the Trials of War Criminals before the Nuremberg Military Tribunals after the war, several doctors were indicted for war crimes for their participation in human experimentation, and those found guilty were sentenced to death. In response to the Nazi testing atrocities, the trial verdict included a set of research principles for human experimentation known as the Nuremberg Code. Although not legally binding, the principles within inspired the human research ethics document developed by the World Medical Association in 1964 known as the Declaration of Helsinki, as well as influenced US federal regulations on human subjects research.

In the United States, a four-decade study regarding medical testing for the treatment of syphilis became a scandal that prompted new concerns about medical testing using human subjects. In 1932, the Public Health Service and the Tuskegee Institute launched the so-called Tuskegee Study of Untreated Syphilis in the Negro Male. The purported goal of the study was to record the disease history of syphilis in order to help develop a treatment program specifically for black men. The study initially involved six hundred black men, two-thirds with syphilis and the rest without it. However, the men were not informed of the purpose of the study but, rather, were told they were being treated for "bad blood," a local term for a variety of illnesses including syphilis. In exchange for participation the men received free medical exams, free meals, and burial insurance. However, they did not in fact receive any treatment for syphilis, even after penicillin became the treatment protocol in 1947. The researchers published papers regarding the health effects of untreated syphilis.

During the 1960s concerns were raised regarding the Tuskegee study, but the US Centers for Disease Control and Prevention, along with chapters of the American Medical Association and National Medical Association, supported continuation of the study. In 1972 news organizations reported on the studies and condemned them, prompting an end to the study forty years after it had begun. In 1974 an out-of-court settlement was reached wherein the US government agreed to provide lifetime medical benefits and burial services to all living participants. That same year, Congress passed the National Research Act establishing the National Commission for the Protection of Human Subjects of Biomedical and Behavioral Research.

Concerns about current medical testing are influenced by past scandals. It is not surprising, given the above examples, that chief among the concerns are that the human subjects are given informed consent and that the possible benefits of the testing outweigh the potential harms.

I *"Clinical trials have gone global and this is certainly a good thing."*

Clinical Trials of New Medical Treatments Need to Be Conducted Globally

Trudie Lang and Sisira Siribaddana

In the following viewpoint, Trudie Lang and Sisira Siribaddana argue that it is necessary for clinical trials to take place around the world, but caution against applying rigid regulations without attention to local difference. Particularly in low- and middle-income countries, the authors claim, there is a need to encourage more local control that yields tangible benefits. Lang is head of the Global Health Network in the Centre for Clinical Vaccinology and Tropical Medicine at the University of Oxford. Siribaddana is a professor of medicine at Rajarata University of Sri Lanka, senior researcher at the Institute of Research and Development, and senior academic with Sri Lankan Twin Registry.

As you read, consider the following questions:

1. The authors identify what "major factor" that explains the increased cost and duration of clinical trials?

Trudie Lang and Sisira Siribaddana, "Clinical Trials Have Gone Global: Is This a Good Thing?," *PLOS Clinical Trials*, vol. 9, no. 6, June 2012, pp. 1–2, 4. Open-Access License, No Permission Required, CCAL 2.5 License, Public Library of Science.

2. The authors claim that increased paperwork and multiple sequential reviews has had what effect on clinical trials in developing countries?

3. According to the authors, what will have to happen to improve the relationship between researchers and the community within developing countries?

Clinical trials are needed globally to reduce disease burdens by helping [in] developing safe and effective new therapies and vaccines. These solutions may be for noncommunicable diseases like cancer and diabetes, or, as is especially needed in the poorest regions of the world, infectious disease. Developing countries are under-represented in research due to lack of commercial viability and trained researchers, yet it is in these poorest regions where research-led solutions could bring the greatest impact to high rates of early mortality.

The Need for Global Clinical Trials

As a research tool clinical trials are fundamental in the effort to develop new products by gaining the data required by regulators, whether for product license extensions for existing therapies for common ailments or to bring cutting edge new therapies and vaccines into approved use. However, there is also a need for clinical trials to bring evidence to determine how to improve the management of health issues; these studies often do not involve a medicinal product but instead compare different options, such as different types of management of an illness in a hospital with community-based care. Or, for example, a clinical trial might be used to assess different mechanisms to improve patient adherence to therapy. These pragmatic disease management trials can bring about significant improvements in public health and often require large yet simple trial designs.

The World Health Organization and journal editors define clinical trials as "any research study that prospectively assigns human participants or groups of humans to one or more health-related interventions to evaluate the effects on health outcomes." Patients may be randomised to an intervention involving either an investigational new product or the standard-of-care treatment, or the patient might be randomised to be cared for by nurses who have been trained in one of two or more comparative ways.

Clinical trial data are often collected from varied populations to support a license application because geographically different trial sites are needed to ensure the product is safe and works in the same way in varying ethnic groups. This requirement is true whether it is a pharmaceutical company working on the next blockbuster drug or a non-for-profit partnership (which typically [has] a pharmaceutical partner involved in a non-for-profit capacity) developing a new drug or vaccine for a neglected disease. Here scientific and regulatory factors combine to encourage the globalisation of clinical trials.

Clinical trials are also being conducted across more diverse countries for economic reasons. Clinical trials are expensive and are taking longer to conduct than in the past, thus further compounding the increased costs, and this is the case for all types of trials, whether commercial or academic. There are many reasons for the increased cost and duration of clinical trials, but it is a widely held view that clinical regulations, or more precisely, the interpretation and implementation of these regulations, are a major factor. Few would argue with the importance of well-regulated clinical trials to ensure high ethical standards and that trial conduct and processes are producing valid and accurate data. However, there is a call for making trial regulation less complicated and more readily adaptable to risk, and for having guidelines that are globally applicable and adaptable to all types of trial. Such guidelines would be as easily applied to pragmatic trials of existing treatments or disease management questions as they would be for trials of new drugs and vaccines.

There are many justifiable reasons for running clinical trials across multiple countries and indeed continents, or even only in sites that are not in the sponsor's location. Some countries are able to recruit participants faster than others for varied and valid reasons. The trial could be for a rare health event, such as dengue fever or traumatic cerebral hemorrhage, and for these trials it is necessary to recruit many centers in diverse locations, each site perhaps recruiting just a few patients to avoid prolonging the duration of the trial and increasing the wait for lifesaving new interventions. It is also true that some regions of the globe are vastly more expensive than others to conduct trials. For example, a clinical trial in India can cost one-tenth of the price that it would cost in the US. Since clinical trials costs are largely driven by labour, much of these savings are from lower salaries to physicians, nurses, and trial coordinators. The time and cost of developing drugs or vaccine influences the final product cost and return on investment, so the logic of reducing trial costs is clear and reasonable.

The Ethical, Scientific, and Operational Challenges of Global Trials

Clinical trials should be designed, conducted, and monitored in proportion to their relative risk and complexity. However, in developing countries it is our experience that external sponsors and their locally appointed contract research organisations (CROs) are often overly zealous in their interpretation of trial guidelines and apply a one-size-fits-all approach to trial coordination and monitoring, irrespective of the risk and complexity. This is often due to an inaccurate perception from the sponsor and/or CRO about the ability of the research sites to run high quality and compliant trials. This perspective can lead to overly cumbersome trials and to burdening of research sites with administrative requests and site visits that are not necessary. In addition, steps and processes are introduced that can alter the expectations of ethics committees, funders, and reviewers and become perpetuated, irrespective of the real need. Many research teams in developing countries do not have the experience to question the necessity of these overly stringent requirements, which therefore remain in place and become the expected norm for every clinical research study.

For example, some ethics committees insist on Data Safety and Monitoring Committees being put in place for every trial even if these committees are not needed or appropriate. However, trials groups often comply without challenging the request, and the requirement becomes a standard step in the process, without examining each time whether it is appropriate for the specific protocol in question. We are not suggesting in any way that processes and standards should be lower or different in developing countries, but we do feel that overly cautious application of regulations is common around the world—and that it creates a greater burden to research in resource-limited settings. . . .

In the US and the UK [United Kingdom] it is increasingly recognised that trials have become too expensive and bureaucratic, and initiatives such as the Clinical Trial Transformation Initiative and the Medical Research Council's Methodology Research Hubs in the UK are trying to rationalise design, conduct, and regulation to improve clinical trial design and make running them easier, more attractive, and less expensive. There is a danger that developing and middle-income countries are not involved in this emerging enthusiasm and effort to make trial design more rational and attractive to potential researchers.

It is essential to protect participants in clinical trials from exploitation and this needs particular care and thought in developing countries where populations can be more vulnerable. To achieve this participant protection, great efforts have been made in recent years to strengthen ethical and regulatory review in developing countries, which is, of course, extremely necessary and important. However, whilst in high-income countries efforts have been made to streamline and simplify ethics and the regulatory review process, application to ethics committees has become highly administrative in resource-limited countries with increasing paper work, and multiple sequential reviews are often needed before a trial can start. This administrative hurdle unfortunately further discourages local academic researchers in developing countries. More wealthy foreign trial sponsors may well have the capacity to resource the administrative burden of getting protocols through these committees; however, low investment and support for ethics and regulatory committees in developing countries is a problem for external sponsors. When international product development efforts are delayed by slow review of trial protocols, this seriously increases the time it takes to develop new drugs and vaccines for diseases of poverty such as tuberculosis and malaria.

The Need for Local Involvement

Clinical trials have gone global and this is certainly a good thing—on the whole. Conducting varying types of trials in low-and middle-income countries (LMICs) can be very positive and the experience research sites gain by working with commercial or not-for-profit sponsors raises research standards and brings health improvements to developing countries and badly needed investment to these research institutions. Externally sponsored trials also bring increasing capacity for research through training and engagement in product development and other global public health initiatives.

However, the global research community needs to improve efforts to support and encourage investigators from LMICs to seek to run their own trials. They need to be provided with incentives and a mandate (possibly from their ministries of health and employing institutions) to plan their own studies and opportunities to diversify beyond externally sponsored trials. A good example of a local investigator-led clinical trial is a recent study in Sri Lanka that addressed a locally relevant question—how to treat snakebites. Interestingly it was advice from a journal's statistician that helped the investigators demonstrate a life-saving intervention to prevent allergic reactions to anti-venom serum for snakebites, which is now being widely used. It is an example of a pragmatic trial that used existing therapies to solve a local issue. The fact that external statistical support was needed shows how capacity is limited and wide support and collaboration are important.

Widespread disparities in clinical care, scientific and health literacy, and economic and social development exist between developed and developing countries. These differences carry concerns about exploitation exacerbated by the power gap between patient-participants and physician-investigators. The vulnerability of developing world patient-participants has been discussed extensively in the past decade.

When running trials in vulnerable populations, such as rural communities in developing countries, detailed consideration needs to be given to engaging with the community, explaining the research that is planned, and then carefully selecting the most appropriate approaches for seeking fully informed consent. More social science-based research is needed to make sure that the best approaches, messages, and methods are being practiced in order to protect the study population (and wider community) and also to ensure that the message is being clearly explained and understood. Do those giving consent really understand what is being asked of them? Do they understand that they have a choice; that they are taking part in research and this differs from standard care and, most importantly, that they can say no?

Clinical trial methodology research is needed because there are great differences in cultures and perceptions across the globe, and what is appropriate in one place might not be in another, and so it might not be appropriate to simply export a

Clinical Research in Developing Countries

Clinical research should be responsive to the health needs and priorities of the communities in which the research is conducted. Given the increasing global prevalence of conditions such as cardiovascular disease, it will be important to test drugs and devices on a global scale. However, among the ongoing phase 3 clinical trials that we examined that were sponsored by U.S.-based companies in developing countries, none were trials of diseases such as tuberculosis that disproportionately affect the populations of these countries. In contrast, we found a variety of trials in developing countries for conditions such as allergic rhinitis and overactive bladder. Developing countries will also not realize the benefits of trials if the drugs being evaluated do not become readily available there once they have been approved.

Seth W. Glickman et al., "Ethical and Scientific Implicationsof the Globalization of Clinical Research," New England Journal of Medicine, *February 19, 2009.*

requirement, and again for this requirement to become introduced unchecked into becoming a standard requirement. For example seeking assent from children is a legal requirement in many countries. Is it always appropriate to apply this rule everywhere? Should a child be asked for assent when they do not normally have any autonomy?

The Importance of Community Trust

There is a need for training and support for clinical trial investigators and their teams, as well as a need for strengthening capacity for scientific and ethical review in these regions. This capacity needs to be cross-cutting and not focused on one disease or protocol if it is to leave trial sites with the skills and knowledge to run their own studies. New globally appropriate guidelines for good clinical practice would greatly benefit researchers working in non-investigational product trials irrespective of where they are in the world. These guidelines need to be informed by internationally based methodology research.

Risk and complexity-based assessment of trials would improve trial conduct, reduce costs, and enable key elements such as quality management to be more likely to pick up real issues that impact trial outcomes, rather than the one-size-fits-all approach to clinical trial monitoring (often described as "tick box checking").

We feel that pre-trial community engagement, ongoing dialogue, and post-trial information giving are important to build and foster community trust for clinical research. Researchers in the developing world should come from the same or similar community and relative standard of living in which the research is being done. Not only would [this] mean they have a sense of belonging to that community and the country, but the country and the community also would own and take pride in their researchers. This relationship will only work if the community receives and perceives tangible and intangible benefits from research. Post-trial access to medicines and devices are an integral part of this creation of trust between researchers and the community. In the case of two clinical trials in Sri Lanka, for example, (one for a snakebite treatment and the other a treatment for yellow oleander poisoning), the products are not available locally because the costs are too high.

In addition we all need to be watchful about exporting mistakes made in the northern hemisphere. Whilst the US and Europe are examining how to encourage more academic trials and limit bureaucracy, these same problems are being applied with extra vigour in less experienced settings. We have found that when there is limited experience, those individuals tasked with reviewing research opt for caution and ask for more rather than less. Whilst this situation is correct and understandable, it highlights the need for research reviewers in developing countries to be better supported and provided with the knowledge and confidence to know which requirements to be applied and when. The current excess of caution is limiting research and making trials more expensive and complex than they need to be. The ramifications are important; too few academic trials and the slow development of new drugs and vaccines in regions of the world most burdened by disease directly impact efforts to reduce early mortality in diseases of poverty.

Finally, the globalisation of clinical trials should not be about running inexpensive trial sites to benefit distant people, but should focus on bringing research to populations who have previously been under-represented in clinical trials, and enabling these same communities the benefits resulting from new drugs, vaccines, and improvements in managing health.

| *"There is no effective chain of command in modern American drug testing."*

Clinical Trials Are Conducted Overseas Without Adequate Oversight

Donald L. Barlett and James B. Steele

In the following viewpoint, Donald L. Barlett and James B. Steele argue that the US government has failed to adequately regulate the globalization of clinical trials by the pharmaceutical industry. The authors claim that the majority of clinical trials are conducted overseas in places where regulation is virtually nonexistent. They contend that because of the gaps in oversight, there are grave concerns about the consent of participants, the safety of trials, the accuracy of research results, and the safety of the pharmaceuticals that are approved as a result of such trials. Barlett and Steele are investigative reporters and contributing editors for Vanity Fair.

As you read, consider the following questions:

1. According to the National Institutes of Health, as reported by Barlett and Steele, how many clinical trials have been conducted outside the United States since 2000?

2. According to the authors, the US Food and Drug Administration visited what fraction of locations of foreign clinical trials in 2008?

3. The authors estimate that the annual US death toll from prescription drugs that are considered safe is what?

You wouldn't think the cities had much in common. Iaşi, with a population of 320,000, lies in the Moldavian region of Romania. Mégrine is a town of 24,000 in northern Tunisia, on the Mediterranean Sea. Tartu, Estonia, with a population of 100,000, is the oldest city in the Baltic States; it is sometimes called "the Athens on the Emajõgi." Shenyang, in northeastern China, is a major industrial center and transportation hub with a population of 7.2 million.

US Clinical Trials Are Moving to Foreign Countries

These places are not on anyone's Top 10 list of travel destinations. But the advance scouts of the pharmaceutical industry have visited all of them, and scores of similar cities and towns, large and small, in far-flung corners of the planet. They have gone there to find people willing to undergo clinical trials for new drugs, and thereby help persuade the U.S. Food and Drug Administration [F.D.A.] to declare the drugs safe and effective for Americans. It's the next big step in globalization, and there's good reason to wish that it weren't.

Once upon a time, the drugs Americans took to treat chronic diseases, clear up infections, improve their state of mind, and enhance their sexual vitality were tested primarily either in the United States (the vast majority of cases) or in Europe. No longer. As recently as 1990, according to the inspector general of the Department of Health and Human Services, a mere 271 trials were being conducted in foreign countries of drugs intended for American use. By 2008, the number had risen to 6,485—an increase of more than 2,000 percent. A database being compiled by the National Institutes of Health has identified 58,788 such trials in 173 countries outside the United States since 2000. In 2008 alone, according to the inspector general's report, 80 percent of the applications submitted to the F.D.A. for new drugs contained data from foreign clinical trials. Increasingly, companies are doing 100 percent of their testing offshore. The inspector general found that the 20 largest U.S.-based pharmaceutical companies now conducted "one-third of their clinical trials exclusively at foreign sites." All of this is taking place when more drugs than ever—some 2,900 different drugs for some 4,600 different conditions—are undergoing clinical testing and vying to come to market.

Some medical researchers question whether the results of clinical trials conducted in certain other countries are relevant to Americans in the first place. They point out that people in impoverished parts of the world, for a variety of reasons, may metabolize drugs differently from the way Americans do. They note that the prevailing diseases in other countries, such as malaria and tuberculosis, can skew the outcome of clinical trials. But from the point of view of the drug companies, it's easy to see why moving clinical trials overseas is so appealing. For one thing, it's cheaper to run trials in places where the local population survives on only a few dollars a day. It's also easier to recruit patients, who often believe they are being treated for a disease rather than, as may be the case, just getting a placebo as part of an experiment. And it's easier to find what the industry calls "drug-naïve" patients: people who are not being treated for any disease and are not currently taking any drugs, and indeed may never have taken any—the sort of people who will almost certainly yield better test results. (For some subjects overseas, participation in a clinical trial may be their first significant exposure to a doctor.) Regulations in many foreign countries are also less stringent, if there are any regulations at all. The risk of litigation is negligible, in some places nonexistent. Ethical concerns are a figure of speech. Finally—a significant plus for the drug companies—the F.D.A. does so little monitoring that the companies can pretty much do and say what they want.

Popular Drug Makers Are Utilizing Overseas Trials

Many of today's trials still take place in developed countries, such as Britain, Italy, and Japan. But thousands are taking place in countries with large concentrations of poor, often illiterate people, who in some cases sign consent forms with a thumbprint, or scratch an "X." Bangladesh has been home to 76 clinical trials. There have been clinical trials in Malawi (61), the Russian Federation (1,513), Romania (876), Thailand (786), Ukraine (589), Kazakhstan (15), Peru (494), Iran (292), Turkey (716), and Uganda (132). Throw a dart at a world map and you are unlikely to hit a spot that has escaped the attention of those who scout out locations for the pharmaceutical industry.

The two destinations that one day will eclipse all the others, including Europe and the United States, are China (with 1,861 trials) and India (with 1,457). A few years ago, India was home to more American drug trials than China was, thanks in part to its large English-speaking population. But that has changed. English is now mandatory in China's elementary schools, and, owing to its population edge, China now has more people who speak English than India does.

While Americans may be unfamiliar with the names of foreign cities where clinical trials have been conducted, many of the drugs being tested are staples of their medicine cabinets. One example is Celebrex, a non-steroidal anti-inflammatory drug that has been aggressively promoted in television commercials for a decade. Its manufacturer, Pfizer, the world's largest drug company, has spent more than a billion dollars promoting its use as a pain remedy for arthritis and other conditions, including menstrual cramps. The National Institutes of Health maintains a record of most—but by no means all—drug trials inside and outside the United States. The database counts 290 studies involving Celebrex. Companies are not required to report—and do not report—all studies conducted overseas. According to the database, of the 290 trials for Celebrex, 183 took place in the United States, meaning, one would assume, that 107 took place in other countries. But an informal, country-by-country accounting by *Vanity Fair* turned up no fewer than 207 Celebrex trials in at least 36 other countries. They ranged from 1 each in Estonia, Croatia, and Lithuania to 6 each in Costa Rica, Colombia, and Russia, to 8 in Mexico, 9 in China, and 10 in Brazil. But even these numbers understate the extent of the foreign trials. For example, the database lists five Celebrex trials in Ukraine, but just "one" of those trials involved studies in 11 different Ukrainian cities.

The Celebrex story does not have a happy ending. First, it was disclosed that patients taking the drug were more likely to suffer heart attacks and strokes than those who took older and cheaper painkillers. Then it was alleged that Pfizer had suppressed a study calling attention to these very problems. (The company denied that the study was undisclosed and insisted that it "acted responsibly in sharing this information in a timely manner with the F.D.A.") Soon afterward the *Journal of the Royal Society of Medicine* reported an array of additional negative findings. Meanwhile, Pfizer was promoting Celebrex for use with Alzheimer's patients, holding out the possibility that the drug would slow the progression of dementia. It didn't. Sales of Celebrex reached $3.3 billion in 2004, and then began to quickly drop.

The Problem with Rescue Countries

One big factor in the shift of clinical trials to foreign countries is a loophole in F.D.A. regulations: if studies in the United

States suggest that a drug has no benefit, trials from abroad can often be used in their stead to secure F.D.A. approval. There's even a term for countries that have shown themselves to be especially amenable when drug companies need positive data fast: they're called "rescue countries." Rescue countries came to the aid of Ketek, the first of a new generation of widely heralded antibiotics to treat respiratory-tract infections. Ketek was developed in the 1990s by Aventis Pharmaceuticals, now Sanofi-Aventis. In 2004—on April Fools' Day, as it happens—the F.D.A. certified Ketek as safe and effective. The F.D.A.'s decision was based heavily on the results of studies in Hungary, Morocco, Tunisia, and Turkey.

The approval came less than one month after a researcher in the United States was sentenced to 57 months in prison for falsifying her own Ketek data. Dr. Anne Kirkman-Campbell, of Gadsden, Alabama, seemingly never met a person she couldn't sign up to participate in a drug trial. She enrolled more than 400 volunteers, about 1 percent of the town's adult population, including her entire office staff. In return, she collected $400 a head from Sanofi-Aventis. It later came to light that the data from at least 91 percent of her patients was falsified. (Kirkman-Campbell was not the only troublesome Aventis researcher. Another physician, in charge of the third-largest Ketek trial site, was addicted to cocaine. The same month his data was submitted to the F.D.A. he was arrested while holding his wife hostage at gunpoint.) Nonetheless, on the basis of overseas trials, Ketek won approval.

As the months ticked by, and the number of people taking the drug climbed steadily, the F.D.A. began to get reports of adverse reactions, including serious liver damage that sometimes led to death. The F.D.A.'s leadership remained steadfast in its support of the drug, but criticism by the agency's own researchers eventually leaked out (a very rare occurrence in this close-knit, buttoned-up world). The critics were especially concerned about an ongoing trial in which 4,000 infants and children, some as young as six months, were recruited in more than a dozen countries for an experiment to assess Ketek's effectiveness in treating ear infections and tonsillitis. The trial had been sanctioned over the objections of the F.D.A.'s own reviewers. One of them argued that the trial never should have been allowed to take place—that it was "inappropriate and unethical because it exposed children to harm without evidence of benefits." In 2006, after inquiries from Congress, the F.D.A. asked Sanofi-Aventis to halt the trial. Less than a year later, one day before the start of a congressional hearing on the F.D.A.'s approval of the drug, the agency suddenly slapped a so-called black-box warning on the label of Ketek, restricting its use. (A black-box warning is the most serious step the F.D.A. can take short of removing a drug from the market.) By then the F.D.A. had received 93 reports of severe adverse reactions to Ketek, resulting in 12 deaths.

During the congressional hearings, lawmakers heard from former F.D.A. scientists who had criticized their agency's oversight of the Ketek trials and the drug-approval process. One was Dr. David Ross, who had been the F.D.A.'s chief reviewer of new drugs for 10 years, and was now the national director of clinical public-health programs for the U.S. Department of Veterans Affairs. When he explained his objections, he offered a litany of reasons that could be applied to any number of other drugs: "Because F.D.A. broke its own rules and allowed Ketek on the market. Because dozens of patients have died or suffered needlessly. Because F.D.A. allowed Ketek's maker to experiment with it on children over reviewers' protests. Because F.D.A. ignored warnings about fraud. And because F.D.A. used data it knew were false to reassure the public about Ketek's safety."

There Is No Chain of Command

To have an effective regulatory system you need a clear chain of command—you need to know who is responsible to whom, all the way up and down the line. There is no effective chain of command in modern American drug testing. Around the time that drugmakers began shifting clinical trials abroad, in the 1990s, they also began to contract out all phases of development and testing, putting them in the hands of for-profit companies. It used to be that clinical trials were done mostly by academic researchers in universities and teaching hospitals, a system that, however imperfect, generally entailed certain minimum standards. The free market has changed all that. Today it is mainly independent contractors who recruit potential patients both in the U.S. and—increasingly—overseas. They devise the rules for the clinical trials, conduct the trials themselves, prepare reports on the results, ghostwrite technical articles for medical journals, and create promotional campaigns. The people doing the work on the front lines are not independent scientists. They are wage-earning technicians who are paid to gather a certain number of human beings; sometimes sequester and feed them; administer certain chemical inputs; and collect samples of urine and blood at regular intervals. The work looks like agribusiness, not research.

What began as a mom-and-pop operation has grown into a vast army of formal "contract-research organizations" that generate annual revenue of $20 billion. They can be found conducting trials in every part of the world. By far the largest is Quintiles Transnational, based in Durham, North Carolina. It offers the services of 23,000 employees in 60 countries, and claims that it has "helped develop or commercialize all of the top 30 best-selling drugs."

Quintiles is privately owned—its investors include two of the U.S.'s top private-equity firms. Other private contractors are public companies, their stock traded on Wall Street. Pharmaceutical Product Development (P.P.D.), a full-service medical contractor based in Wilmington, North Carolina, is a public company with 10,500 employees. It, too, has conducted clinical trials all around the world. In fact, it was involved in the clinical trials for Ketek—a P.P.D. research associate, Ann Marie Cisneros, had been assigned to monitor Dr. Anne Kirkman-Campbell's testing in Alabama. Cisneros later told the congressional investigating committee that Kirkman-Campbell had indeed engaged in fraud. "But what the court that sentenced her did not know," Cisneros said, was that "Aventis was not a victim of this fraud." Cisneros said she had reported her findings of fraud to her employer, P.P.D., and also to Aventis. She told the congressional committee, "What brings me here today is my disbelief at Aventis's statements that it did not know that fraud was being committed. Mr. Chairman, I knew it, P.P.D. knew it, and Aventis knew it." Following her testimony the company released a statement saying it regretted the violations that occurred during the study but was not aware of the fraud until after the data was submitted to the F.D.A.

There Is a Lack of Federal Oversight

The F.D.A., the federal agency charged with oversight of the food and drugs that Americans consume, is rife with conflicts of interest. Doctors who insist the drug you take is perfectly safe maybe collecting hundreds of thousands of dollars from the company selling the drug. (ProPublica, an independent, nonprofit news organization that is compiling an ongoing catalogue of pharmaceutical-company payments to physicians, has identified 17,000 doctors who have collected speaking and consulting fees, including nearly 400 who have received $100,000 or more since 2009.) Quite often, the F.D.A. never bothers to check for interlocking financial interests. In one study, the agency failed to document the financial interests of applicants in 31 percent of applications for new-drug approval. Even when the agency or the company knew of a potential conflict of interest, neither acted to guard against bias in the test results.

Because of the deference shown to drug companies by the F.D.A.—and also by Congress, which has failed to impose any meaningful regulation—there is no mandatory public record of the results of drug trials conducted in foreign countries. Nor is there any mandatory public oversight of ongoing trials. If one company were to test an experimental drug that killed more patients than it helped, and kept the results secret, another company might unknowingly repeat the same experiment years later, with the same results. Data is made available to the public on a purely voluntary basis. Its accuracy is unknown. The oversight that does exist often is shot through with the kinds of ethical conflicts that Wall Street would admire. The economic incentives for doctors in poor countries to heed the wishes of the drug companies are immense. An executive at a contract-research organization told the anthropologist Adriana Petryna, author of the book *When Experiments Travel*: "In Russia, a doctor makes two hundred dollars a month, and he is going to make five thousand dollars per Alzheimer's patient" that he signs up. Even when the most flagrant conflicts are disclosed, penalties are minimal. In truth, the same situation exists in the United States. There's just more of a chance here, though not a very large one, that adverse outcomes and tainted data will become public. When the pharmaceutical industry insists that its drugs have been tested overseas in accordance with F.D.A. standards, this may be true—but should provide little assurance.

The F.D.A. gets its information on foreign trials almost entirely from the companies themselves. It conducts little or no independent research. The investigators contracted by the pharmaceutical companies to manage clinical trials are left pretty much on their own. In 2008 the F.D.A. inspected just 1.9 percent of trial sites inside the United States to ensure that they were complying with basic standards. Outside the country, it inspected even fewer trial sites—seven-tenths of 1 percent. In 2008, the F.D.A. visited only 45 of the 6,485 locations where foreign drug trials were being conducted. . . .

The Need for Government Regulation

The only people who seem to care about the surge of clinical trials in foreign countries are the medical ethicists—not historically a powerhouse when it comes to battling the drug companies. A team of physician-researchers from Duke University, writing last year [2010] in the *New England Journal of Medicine*, observed that "this phenomenon raises important questions about the economics and ethics of clinical research and the translation of trial results to clinical practice: Who benefits from the globalization of clinical trials? What is the potential for exploitation of research subjects? Are trial results accurate and valid, and can they be extrapolated to other settings?" The Duke team noted that, in some places, "financial compensation for research participation may exceed participants' annual wages, and participation in a clinical trial may provide the only access to care" for those taking part in the trial. In 2007, residents of a homeless shelter in Grudziadz, Poland, received as little as $2 to take part in a flu-vaccine experiment. The subjects thought they were getting a regular flu shot. They were not. At least 20 of them died. The same distorting economic pressures exist for local hospitals or doctors, who may collect hundreds of dollars for every patient they enroll. In theory, a federal institutional review board is supposed to assess every clinical trial, with special concern for the welfare of the human subjects, but this work, too, has now been outsourced to private companies and is often useless. In 2009 the Government Accountability Office conducted a sting operation, winning approval for a clinical trial involving human subjects; the institutional review board failed to discover (if it even tried) that it was dealing with "a bogus company with falsified credentials" and a fake medical device. This was in Los Angeles. If that is oversight in the U.S., imagine what it's like in Kazakhstan or Uganda. Susan Reverby, the Wellesley historian who uncovered the U.S. government's syphilis experiments in Guatemala during the 1940s, was asked in a recent interview to cite any ongoing experimental practices that gave her pause. "Frankly," she said, "I am mostly worried about the drug trials that get done elsewhere now, which we have little control over."

The pharmaceutical industry, needless to say, has a different view. It argues that people participating in a clinical trial may be getting the highest quality of medical care they have ever received. That may be true in the short term. But, unfortunately, the care lasts only until the trial is completed. Many U.S. medical investigators who manage drug trials abroad say they prefer to work overseas, where regulations are lax and "conflict of interest" is a synonym for "business as usual." Inside the United States, doctors who oversee trials are required to fill out forms showing any income they have received from drug companies so as to guard against financial biases in trials. This explains in part why the number of clinical-trial investigators registered with the F.D.A. fell 5.2 percent in the U.S. between 2004 and 2007 while increasing 16 percent in Eastern Europe, 12 percent in Asia, and 10 percent in Latin America. In a recent survey, 70 percent of the eligible U.S. and Western European clinical investigators interviewed said they were discouraged by the current regulatory environment, partly because they are compelled to disclose financial ties to the pharmaceutical industry. In trials conducted outside the United States, few people care.

In 2009, according to the Institute for Safe Medication Practices, 19,551 people died in the United States as a direct result of the prescription drugs they took. That's just the reported number. It's decidedly low, because it is estimated that only about 10 percent of such deaths are reported. Conservatively, then, the annual American death toll from prescription drugs considered "safe" can be put at around 200,000. That is three times the number of people who die every year from diabetes, four times the number who die from kidney disease. Overall, deaths from F.D.A.-approved prescription drugs dwarf the number of people who die from street drugs such as co-caine and heroin. They dwarf the number who die every year in automobile accidents. So far, these deaths have triggered no medical crusades, no tough new regulations. After a dozen or so deaths linked to runaway Toyotas, Japanese executives were summoned to appear before lawmakers in Washington and were subjected to an onslaught of humiliating publicity. When the pharmaceutical industry meets with lawmakers, it is mainly to provide campaign contributions.

And with more and more of its activities moving overseas, the industry's behavior will become more impenetrable, and more dangerous, than ever.

> "Groundbreaking scientific advances in the present and the past were possible only because of participation of volunteers ... in clinical research."

Volunteers Are Critical to Advancing Medicine Through Clinical Trials

National Institutes of Health

In the following viewpoint, the National Institutes of Health (NIH) contends that scientific advances in the field of medicine are possible through clinical trials, which test the safety and effectiveness of drugs and therapies. NIH claims that such trials are possible only with the participation of both healthy volunteers and volunteers with illnesses that may be helped by such participation. NIH argues that clinical trials are governed by ethical guidelines that protect volunteers and preserve scientific outcomes. NIH, part of the US Department of Health and Human Services, is the nation's medical research agency.

As you read, consider the following questions:

1. According to the NIH, each clinical trial in the United States must be approved and monitored by an institutional review board to ensure what?

National Institutes of Health, "NIH Clinical Research Trials and You: The Basics," October 15, 2012.

2. Clinical trials need what two types of volunteers, according to the NIH?

3. According to the NIH, institutional review boards are independent committees that consist of whom?

Clinical trials are part of clinical research and at the heart of all medical advances. Clinical trials look at new ways to prevent, detect, or treat disease. Treatments might be new drugs or new combinations of drugs, new surgical procedures or devices, or new ways to use existing treatments. The goal of clinical trials is to determine if a new test or treatment works and is safe. Clinical trials can also look at other aspects of care, such as improving the quality of life for people with chronic illnesses.

People participate in clinical trials for a variety of reasons. Healthy volunteers say they participate to help others and to contribute to moving science forward. Participants with an illness or disease also participate to help others, but also to possibly receive the newest treatment and to have the additional care and attention from the clinical trial staff. Clinical trials offer hope for many people and an opportunity to help researchers find better treatments for others in the future.

How Clinical Research Is Conducted

Clinical research is medical research that involves people like you. People volunteer to participate in carefully conducted investigations that ultimately uncover better ways to treat, prevent, diagnose, and understand human disease. Clinical research includes trials that test new treatments and therapies as well as long-term natural history studies, which provide valuable information about how disease and health progress.

The idea for a clinical research study—also known as a clinical trial—often originates in the laboratory. After researchers test new therapies or procedures in the laboratory and in animal studies, the most promising experimental treatments are moved into clinical trials, which are conducted in phases. During a trial, more information is gained about an experimental treatment, its risks, and its effectiveness.

Clinical research is conducted according to a plan known as a protocol. The protocol is carefully designed to safeguard the participants' health and answer specific research questions. A protocol describes the following:

- Who is eligible to participate in the trial

- Details about tests, procedures, medications, and dosages

- The length of the study and what information will be gathered

A clinical study is led by a principal investigator (PI), who is often a doctor. Members of the research team regularly monitor the participants' health to determine the study's safety and effectiveness.

Each clinical trial in the United States must be approved and monitored by an Institutional Review Board (IRB) to ensure that the risks are minimal and are worth any potential benefits. An IRB is an independent committee that consists of physicians, statisticians, and members of the community who ensure that clinical trials are ethical and that the rights of participants are protected. Federal regulation requires all institutions in the United States that conduct or support biomedical research involving people to have an IRB initially approve and periodically review the research.

Clinical trials are sponsored or funded by various organizations or individuals, including physicians, foundations, medical institutions, voluntary groups, and pharmaceutical companies, as well as federal agencies such as the National Institutes of Health and the Department of Veterans Affairs.

Informed consent is the process of providing potential participants with the key facts about a clinical trial before they decide whether to participate. The process of informed consent (providing additional information) continues throughout the study. To help someone decide whether or not to participate, members of the research team explain the details of the study. Translation or interpretive assistance can be provided for participants with limited English proficiency. The research team provides an informed consent document that includes details about the study, such as its purpose, duration, required procedures, and who to contact for further information. The informed consent document also explains risks and potential benefits. The participant then decides whether to sign the document. Informed consent is not a contract. Volunteers are free to withdraw from the study completely or to refuse particular treatments or tests at any time. Sometimes, however, this will make them ineligible to continue the study.

Types and Phases of Clinical Trials

There are different types of clinical trials.

- *Natural history studies* provide valuable information about how disease and health progress.

- *Prevention trials* look for better ways to prevent a disease in people who have never had the disease or to prevent the disease from returning. Better approaches may include medicines, vaccines, or lifestyle changes, among other things.

- *Screening trials* test the best way to detect certain diseases or health conditions.

- *Diagnostic trials* determine better tests or procedures for diagnosing a particular disease or condition.

- *Treatment trials* test new treatments, new combinations of drugs, or new approaches to surgery or radiation therapy.

- *Quality of life trials* (or supportive care trials) explore and measure ways to improve the comfort and quality of life of people with a chronic illness.

Clinical trials are conducted in "phases." Each phase has a different purpose and helps researchers answer different questions.

- *Phase I trials*: Researchers test an experimental drug or treatment in a small group of people (20–80) for the first time. The purpose is to evaluate its safety and identify side effects.

- *Phase II trials*: The experimental drug or treatment is administered to a larger group of people (100–300) to determine its effectiveness and to further evaluate its safety.

- *Phase III trials*: The experimental drug or treatment is administered to large groups of people (1,000–3,000) to confirm its effectiveness, monitor side effects, compare it with standard or equivalent treatments, and collect information that will allow the experimental drug or treatment to be used safely.

- *Phase IV trials*: After a drug is approved by the FDA and made available to the public, researchers track its safety, seeking more information about a drug or treatment's risks, benefits, and optimal use.

Typically, clinical trials compare a new product or therapy with another that already exists to determine if the new one is as successful as, or better than, the existing one. In some studies, participants may be assigned to receive a *placebo* (an inactive product that resembles the test product, but without its treatment value).

Comparing a new product with a placebo can be the fastest and most reliable way to demonstrate the new product's therapeutic effectiveness. However, placebos are not used if a patient would be put at risk—particularly in the study of treatments for serious illnesses—by not having effective therapy. Most of these studies compare new products with an approved therapy. Potential participants are told if placebos will be used in the study before they enter a trial.

Randomization is the process by which two or more alternative treatments are assigned to volunteers by chance rather than by choice. This is done to avoid any bias with investigators assigning volunteers to one group or another. The results of each treatment are compared at specific points during a trial, which may last for years. When one treatment is found superior, the trial is stopped so that the fewest volunteers receive the less beneficial treatment.

In *single- or double-blind studies*, also called single- or double-masked studies, the participants do not know which medicine is being used, so they can describe what happens without bias. "Blind" (or "masked") studies are designed to prevent members of the research team or study participants from influencing the results. This allows scientifically accurate conclusions. In single-blind ("single-masked") studies, only the patient is not told what is being administered. In a double-blind study, only the pharmacist knows; members of the research team are not told which patients are getting which medication, so that their observations will not be biased. If medically necessary, however, it is always possible to find out what the patient is taking.

Who Participates in Clinical Trials?

Many different types of people participate in clinical trials. Some are healthy, while others may have illnesses. A *healthy volunteer* is a person with no known significant health problems who participates in clinical research to test a new drug, device, or intervention. Research procedures with healthy volunteers are designed to develop new knowledge, not to pro-

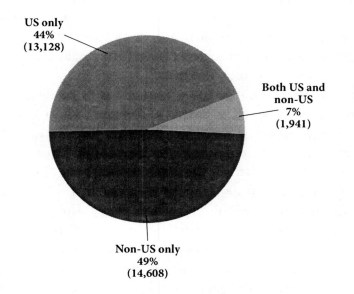

Locations of Recruiting Clinical Trials in 2013

Distribution of locations for recruiting studies registered on ClinicalTrials.gov.

US only
44%
(13,128)

Both US and
non-US
7%
(1,941)

Non-US only
49%
(14,608)

TAKEN FROM: US National Institutes of Health, "Trends, Charts, and Maps," ClinicalTrials.gov, February 2013.

vide direct benefit to study participants. Healthy volunteers have always played an important role in research.

Healthy volunteers are needed for several reasons. When developing a new technique, such as a blood test or imaging device, healthy volunteers (formerly called "normal volunteers") help define the limits of "normal." These volunteers serve as controls for patient groups and are often matched to patients on characteristics such as age, gender, or family relationship. They receive the same test, procedure, or drug the patient group receives. Investigators learn about the disease process by comparing the patient group to the healthy volunteers.

Factors like how much of your time is needed, discomfort you may feel, or risk involved depends on the trial. While some require minimal amounts of time and effort, other studies may require a major commitment in time and effort on behalf of the volunteer, and may involve some discomfort. The research procedure may also carry some risk. The consent process for healthy volunteers includes a detailed discussion of the study's procedures and tests.

A *patient volunteer* has a known health problem and participates in research to better understand, diagnose, treat, or cure that disease or condition. Research procedures with a patient volunteer help develop new knowledge. These procedures may or may not benefit the study participants.

Patient volunteers may be involved in studies similar to those in which healthy volunteers participate. These studies involve drugs, devices, or interventions designed to prevent, treat, or cure disease. Although these studies may provide direct benefit to patient volunteers, the main aim is to prove, by scientific means, the effects and limitations of the experimental treatment. Consequently, some patients serve as controls by not taking the test drug, or by receiving test doses of the drug large enough only to show that it is present, but not at a level that can treat the condition. A study's benefits may be indirect for the volunteers but may help others. . . .

The Risks and Benefits of Clinical Research

The goal of clinical research is to develop knowledge that improves human health or increases understanding of human biology.

People who participate in clinical research make it possible for this to occur. The path to finding out if a new drug is safe or effective is to test it on patient volunteers. By placing some people at risk of harm for the good of others, clinical research has the potential to exploit patient volunteers. The purpose of ethical guidelines is both to protect patient volunteers and to preserve the integrity of the science. Ethical guidelines in place today were primarily a response to past research abuses.

Informed consent is the process of learning the key facts about a clinical trial before deciding whether to participate. The process of providing information to participants continues throughout the study. To help someone decide whether to participate, members of the research team explain details of the study. The research team provides an informed consent document, which includes such details about the study as its purpose, duration, required procedures, and who to contact for various purposes. The informed consent document also explains risks and potential benefits.

If the participant decides to enroll in the trial, the informed consent document will be signed. Informed consent is not a contract. Volunteers are free to withdraw from the study at any time.

Each clinical trial in the United States must be approved and monitored by an Institutional Review Board (IRB) to ensure that the risks are minimal and are worth any potential benefits. An IRB is an independent committee that consists of physicians, statisticians, and members of the community who ensure that clinical trials are ethical and that the rights of participants are protected. Federal regulation requires all institutions in the United States that conduct or support biomedical research involving people to have an IRB initially approve and periodically review the research.

The Outcomes of Clinical Trials

After a clinical trial is completed, the researchers carefully examine information collected during the study before making decisions about the meaning of the findings and about further testing. After a phase I or II trial, the researchers decide whether to move on to the next phase or to stop testing the agent or intervention because it was unsafe or ineffective.

When a phase III trial is completed, the researchers examine the data and decide whether the results have medical importance.

Results from clinical trials are often published in peer-reviewed scientific journals. *Peer review* is a process by which experts review the report before it is published to ensure that the analysis and conclusions are sound. If the results are particularly important, they may be featured in news media and discussed at scientific meetings and by patient advocacy groups before they are published. Once a new approach has been proven safe and effective in a clinical trial, it may become the standard of medical practice. . . .

Only through clinical research can we gain insights and answers about the safety and effectiveness of drugs and therapies. Groundbreaking scientific advances in the present and the past were possible only because of participation of volunteers, both healthy and those diagnosed with an illness, in clinical research. Clinical research requires complex and rigorous testing in collaboration with communities that are affected by the disease. As clinical research opens new doors to finding ways to diagnose, prevent, treat, or cure disease and disability, clinical trial participation of volunteers is essential to help us find the answers.

| "The relationship between testers and test subjects has become, more nakedly than ever, a business transaction."

Paying Human Research Subjects Raises Ethical Concerns

Carl Elliott

In the following viewpoint, Carl Elliott argues that the rise in so-called professional guinea pigs—people who get paid to be human research subjects as a job—raises ethical concerns. Elliott claims that the lack of governmental oversight and the relative powerlessness of the human subject population support the current medical testing environment where scandal and disaster are all too common. Elliott is a professor in the Center for Bioethics and the departments of pediatrics and philosophy at the University of Minnesota. He is author of White Coat, Black Hat: Adventures on the Dark Side of Medicine.

As you read, consider the following questions:

1. According to the author, what was different about the way clinical trials were conducted in 1991, compared to now?

2. Elliott claims that in recent years what change has come to the way in which institutional review boards function?

3. In what way does the perspective of professional guinea pigs on the issue of payment differ from that of ethicists and regulators, according to the author?

Most drug studies used to take place in medical schools and teaching hospitals.

Pharmaceutical companies developed the drugs, but they contracted with academic physicians to carry out the clinical testing. According to The *New England Journal of Medicine*, as recently as 1991 eighty per cent of industry-sponsored trials were conducted in academic health centers. Academic health centers had a lot to offer pharmaceutical companies: academic researchers who could design the trials, publications in academic journals that could help market the products, and a pool of potential subjects on whom the drugs could be tested. But, in the past decade, the pharmaceutical industry has been testing more drugs, the trials have grown more complex, and the financial pressure to bring drugs to market swiftly has intensified. Impatient with the slow pace of academic bureaucracies, pharmaceutical companies have moved trials to the private sector, where more than seventy per cent of them are now conducted.

The Rise of Professional Guinea Pigs

This has spurred the growth of businesses that specialize in various parts of the commercial-research enterprise. The largest of the new businesses are called "contract research organizations," and include Quintiles, Covance, Parexel, and P.P.D. (Pharmaceutical Product Development), a company that has operations in thirty countries, including India, Israel, and South Africa. (About fifty per cent of clinical trials are now conducted outside the United States and Western Europe.)

These firms are hired to shepherd a product through every aspect of its development, from subject recruitment and testing through F.D.A. [US Food and Drug Administration] approval. Speed is critical: a patent lasts twenty years, and a drug company's aim is to get the drug on the shelves as early in the life of the patent as possible. When, in 2000, the Office of the Inspector General of the Department of Health and Human Services asked one researcher what sponsors were looking for, he replied, "No. 1—rapid enrollment. No. 2—rapid enrollment. No. 3—rapid enrollment." The result has been to broaden the range of subjects who are used and to increase the rates of pay they receive.

Most professional guinea pigs are involved in Phase I clinical trials, in which the safety of a potential drug is tested, typically by giving it to healthy subjects and studying any side effects that it produces. (Phase II trials aim at determining dosing requirements and demonstrating therapeutic efficacy; Phase III trials are on a larger scale and usually compare a drug's results with standard treatments.) The better trial sites offer such amenities as video games, pool tables, and wireless Internet access. If all goes well, a guinea pig can get paid to spend a week watching "The Lord of the Rings" and playing Halo with his friends, in exchange for wearing a hep-lock catheter on one arm and eating institutional food. Nathaniel Miller, a Philadelphia trial veteran who started doing studies to fund his political activism, was once paid fifteen hundred dollars in exchange for three days and two G.I. [gastrointestinal] endoscopies at Temple University, where he was given a private room with a television. "It was like a hotel," he says, "except that twice they came in and stuck a tube down my nose."

The shift to the market has created a new dynamic. The relationship between testers and test subjects has become, more nakedly than ever, a business transaction. Guinea pigs are the first to admit this. "Nobody's doing this out of the

"Human guinea pigs...I find that insulting!"

© Joseph Farris/www.CartoonStock.com.

goodness of their heart," Miller says. Unlike subjects in later-stage clinical trials, who are usually sick and might enroll in a study to gain access to a new drug, people in healthy-volunteer studies cannot expect any therapeutic benefit to balance the risks they take. As guinea pigs see it, their reason for taking the drugs is no different from that of the clinical investigators who administer them, and who are compensated handsomely for their efforts. This raises an ethical question: what happens when both parties involved in a trial see the enterprise primarily as a way of making money?

Examining Drug-Testing Site Scandals

In May of 2006, Miami-Dade County ordered the demolition of a former Holiday Inn, citing various fire and safety violations. It had been the largest drug-testing site in North America, with six hundred and seventy-five beds. The operation closed down that year, shortly after the financial magazine *Bloomberg Markets* reported that the building's owner, SFBC International, was paying undocumented immigrants to participate in drug trials under ethically dubious conditions. The medical director of the clinic got her degree from a school in the Caribbean and was not licensed to practice. Some of the studies had been approved by a commercial ethical-review board owned by the wife of an SFBC vice-president. (The company, which has since changed its name to PharmaNet Development Group, says that it required subjects to provide proof of their legal status, and that the practice of medicine wasn't part of the medical director's duties. Last August [2007], the company paid $28.5 million to settle a class-action lawsuit.)

"It was a human-subjects bazaar," says Kenneth Goodman, a bioethicist at the University of Miami who visited the site. The motel was in a downtrodden neighborhood; according to later reports, paint was peeling from the walls, and there were seven or eight subjects in a room. Goodman says that the waiting area was filled with potential subjects, mainly African-American and Hispanic; administrative staff members worked behind a window, like gas-station attendants, passing documents through a hole in the glass.

The SFBC scandal was not the first of its kind. In 1996, the *Wall Street Journal* reported that the Eli Lilly company was using homeless alcoholics from a local shelter to test experimental drugs at budget rates at its testing site in Indianapolis. (Lilly's executive director of clinical pharmacology told the *Journal* that the homeless people were driven by "altruism," and that they enrolled in trials because they "want to help society." The company says that it now requires subjects to provide proof of residence.) The Lilly clinic, the *Journal* reported, had developed such a reputation for admitting the down-and-out that subjects travelled to Indianapolis from all over the country to participate in studies.

There Is a Lack of Oversight

How did the largest clinical-trial unit on the continent recruit undocumented immigrants to a dilapidated motel for ten years without anyone noticing? Part of the answer has to do with our system of oversight. Before the nineteen-seventies, medical research was poorly regulated; many Phase I subjects were prisoners. Reforms were instituted after congressional investigations into abuses like the four-decade Tuskegee syphilis studies, in which researchers studied, instead of treating, syphilis infections in African-American men. For the past three decades, institutional review boards, or I.R.B.s, have been the primary mechanism for protecting subjects in drug trials. F.D.A. regulations require that any study in support of a new drug be approved by an I.R.B. Until recently, I.R.B.s were based in universities and teaching hospitals, and were made up primarily of faculty members who volunteered to review the research studies being conducted in their own institutions. Now that most drug studies take place outside academic settings, research sponsors can submit their proposed studies to for-profit I.R.B.s, which will review the ethics of a study in exchange for a fee. These boards are subject to the same financial pressures faced by virtually everyone in the business. They compete for clients by promising a fast review. And if one for-profit I.R.B. concludes that a study is unethical the sponsor can simply take it to another.

Moreover, because I.R.B.s scrutinize studies only on paper, they are seldom in a position to comment on conditions at a study site. Most of the standards that SFBC violated in Miami, for example, would not be covered in an ordinary off-site ethics review. I.R.B.s ask questions like "Have the subjects been adequately informed of what the study involves?" They do not generally ask if the sponsors are recruiting undocumented immigrants or if the study site poses a fire hazard. At some trial sites, guinea pigs are housed in circumstances that would drive away anyone with better options. Guinea pigs told me about sites that skimp on meals and hot water, or that require subjects to bring their own towels and blankets. A few sites have a reputation for recruiting subjects who are threatening or dangerous but work cheaply.

Few people realize how little oversight the federal government provides for the protection of subjects in privately sponsored studies. The Office for Human Research Protections, in the Department of Health and Human Services, has jurisdiction only over research funded by the department. The F.D.A. oversees drug safety, but, according to a 2007 H.H.S. report, it conducts "more inspections that verify clinical trial data than inspections that focus on human-subject protections." In 2005, F.D.A. inspectors were finally given a code number for reporting "failure to protect the rights, safety, and welfare of subjects," and an agency spokesman says that they plan to make more human-subject-safety inspections in the future, but so far they have cited only one investigator for a violation. (He had held a subject in his research unit against her will.) In any case, the F.D.A. inspects only about one per cent of clinical trials.

A Look at Recent Testing Disasters

Most guinea pigs rely on their wits—or on word of mouth from other subjects—to determine which studies are safe. Some avoid particular kinds of studies, such as trials for heart drugs or psychiatric drugs. Others have developed relationships with certain recruiters, whom they trust to tell them which studies to avoid. In general, guinea pigs figure that sponsors have a financial incentive to keep them healthy. "The companies don't give two shits about me or my personal well-being," Nathaniel Miller says. "But it's not in their interest for anything to go wrong." That's true, but companies also have an interest in things going well as cheaply as possible, and this can lead to hazardous tradeoffs.

The most notorious recent disaster for healthy volunteers took place in March, 2006, at a testing site run by Parexel at Northwick Park Hospital, outside London; subjects were offered two thousand pounds to enroll in a Phase I trial of a monoclonal antibody, a prospective treatment for rheumatoid arthritis and multiple sclerosis. Six of the volunteers had to be rushed to a nearby intensive-care unit after suffering life-threatening reactions—severe inflammation, organ failure. They were hospitalized for weeks, and one subject's fingers and toes were amputated. All the subjects have reportedly been left with long-term disabilities.

The Northwick Park episode was not an isolated incident. Traci Johnson, a previously healthy nineteen-year-old student, committed suicide in a safety study of Eli Lilly's antidepressant Cymbalta in January of 2004. (Lilly denies that its product was to blame.) I spoke to an Iraqi living in Canada who began doing trials when he immigrated. He was living in a hostel and needed money to buy a car. A friend told him, "This thing is like fast cash." When he enrolled in an immunosuppressant trial at a Montreal-based subsidiary of SFBC, he found himself in a bed next to a subject who was coughing up blood. Despite his complaints, he was not moved to a different bed for nine days. He and eight other subjects later tested positive for tuberculosis. . . .

The Growth of Guinea-Pig Activism

[Bob] Helms is a pioneer in the world of guinea-pig activism. A fifty-year-old housepainter and former union organizer, he has a calm, measured demeanor that masks a deep dissident streak. Before he started guinea-pigging, in the nineteen-nineties, he worked as a caregiver for mentally retarded adults living in group homes. There Helms began to understand the difficulties in organizing health-care workers who were employed by the same company but in far-flung locations—in this case, group homes that were spread over two hundred miles of suburbs. "The other organizers told me right off the bat that I could not organize workers who might meet each other once a year at best," Helms says. "How could we ask them to take risks together? They were strangers."

Helms saw that guinea pigs faced a similar problem, and, in 1996, he started a jobzine for research subjects called *Guinea Pig Zero*. With a mixture of reporting, advocacy, and dark humor (a cartoon in an early issue shows a young man surrounded by I.V. [intravenous] bags and syringes, exclaiming, "No more fast food work for me—I've got a career in science!"), *Guinea Pig Zero* published the sort of information that guinea pigs really wanted to know—how well a study paid, the competence of the venipuncturist, the quality of the food. It even published report cards, grading research units from A to F. "Overcrowding, no hot showers, sleeping in an easy chair, incredibly cheap shit for dinner, creepy guys from New York jails—all these are a poor man's worries," Helms says. "Where are these things in the regulators' paperwork?" *Guinea Pig Zero* was not aimed at sick people who sign up for studies in order to get new treatment. It was aimed at poor people who sign up for studies in order to get money.

And here is where its perspective diverged most radically from the traditional ethical perspective. *Guinea Pig Zero* assumed that subjects should get more money, while many ethicists and regulators argued that they should get none at all. The standard worry expressed by ethicists is that money tempts subjects to take part in dangerous, painful, or degrading studies against their better judgment. F.D.A. guidelines instruct review boards to make sure that payment is not "coercive" and does not exert an "undue influence" on subjects. It's a reasonable worry. "If there were a study where they cut off your leg and sewed it back on and you got twenty thousand dollars, people would be fighting to get into that study," a Philadelphia activist and clinical-trial veteran who writes under the name Dave Onion says.

Should Research Subjects Be Paid?

Of course, ethicists generally prefer that subjects take part in studies for altruistic reasons. Yet, if sponsors relied solely on altruism, studies on healthy subjects would probably come to a halt. The result is an uneasy compromise: guinea pigs are paid to test drugs, but everyone pretends that guinea-pigging is not really a job. I.R.B.s allow sponsors to pay guinea pigs, but, consistent with F.D.A. guidelines, insist on their keeping the amount low. Sponsors refer to the money as "compensation" rather than as "wages," but guinea pigs must pay taxes, and they are given no retirement benefits, disability insurance, workmen's compensation, or overtime pay. And, because so many guinea pigs are uninsured, they are testing the safety of drugs that they will probably not be able to afford once the drugs have been approved. "I'm not going to get the benefit of the health care that is developed by this research," Helms says, "because I am not in the economic class to get health insurance."

Guinea pigs can't even count on having their medical care paid for if they are injured in a study. According to a recent survey in The *New England Journal of Medicine,* only sixteen per cent of academic medical centers in the United States provided free care to subjects injured in trials. None of them compensated injured subjects for pain or lost wages. No systematic data are available for private testing sites, but the provisions typically found in consent forms are not encouraging. A consent form for a recent study of Genentech's immunosuppressant drug Raptiva told participants that they would be treated for any injuries the drug caused, but stipulated that "the cost of such treatment will not be reimbursed."

Some sponsors withhold most of the payment until the studies are over. Guinea pigs who drop out after deciding that a surgical procedure is too disagreeable, or that a drug seems unpleasant or dangerous, must forfeit the bulk of their paycheck. Two years ago, when SFBC conducted a two-month study of the pain medication Palladone, it offered subjects twenty-four hundred dollars. But most of that was paid only after the last of the study's four confinement periods. A guinea pig could spend nearly two months in the study, including twelve days and nights in the SFBC unit, and get only six hundred dollars. SFBC even reserved the right to withhold payments from subjects whom it dropped from the study because of a drug's side effects.

The Unsafe World of Guinea-Pigging

Guinea-pig activists recognize that they are indispensable to the pharmaceutical industry; a guinea-pig walkout in the middle of a trial could wreak financial havoc on the sponsor. Yet the conditions of guinea-pigging make any exercise of power difficult. Not only are those in a particular trial likely to be strangers; if they complain to the sponsor about conditions, they risk being excluded from future studies. And, according to *Bloomberg*, when illegal-immigrant guinea pigs at SFBC talked to the press, managers threatened to have them deported. . . .

Perhaps there is something inherently disconcerting about the idea of turning drug testing into a job. Guinea pigs do not do things in exchange for money so much as they allow things to be done to them. There are not many other jobs where that is the case. Meanwhile, our patchwork regulatory system insures that no one institution is keeping track of how many deaths and injuries befall healthy subjects in clinical trials. Nobody appears to be tracking how many clinical investigators are incompetent, or have lost their licenses, or have questionable disciplinary records. Nobody is monitoring the effect that so many trials have on the health of professional guinea pigs. In fact, nobody is even entirely certain whether the trials generate reliable data. A professional guinea pig who does a dozen drug-safety trials a year is not exactly representative of the population that will be taking the drugs once they have been approved.

The safety of new drugs has always depended on the willingness of someone to test them, and it seems inevitable that the job will fall to people who have no better options. Guinea-pigging requires no training or skill, and in a thoroughly commercial environment, where there can be no pretense of humanitarian motivation, it is hard to think of it as meaningful work. As Dave Onion puts it, "You don't go home and say to yourself, 'Now, that was a good day.'"

> *"By focusing so intently on one organism, raised in a certain way, we may be limiting our knowledge of . . . the causes of death for many millions of people every year."*

Rodents Are Overused as Subjects in Medical Research

Daniel Engber

In the following viewpoint, Daniel Engber argues that scientists are starting to come to the conclusion that rats and mice are too frequently used as research subjects for testing medical devices and treatments intended for humans. Engber claims that there are a variety of reasons that rodents do not always make good test subjects, including the fact that lab rodents are often over-weight and sedentary, as well as the fact that diseases such as tuberculosis do not act the same upon mice and humans. Engber writes and edits science coverage for Slate.

As you read, consider the following questions:

1. The author claims that according to the European Union, in 2008 rats and mice accounted for what fraction of animals used for experiments?

2. According to Engber, scientist Clif Barry claims that before compounds are tested in humans, in what two places must they first be tested?

3. What major difference exists between tuberculosis in mice and tuberculosis in humans, according to the author?

Mark Mattson knows a lot about mice and rats. He's fed them; he's bred them; he's cut their heads open with a scalpel. Over a brilliant 25-year career in neuroscience—one that's made him a Laboratory Chief at the National Institute on Aging, a professor of neuroscience at Johns Hopkins, a consultant to Alzheimer's nonprofits, and a leading scholar of degenerative brain conditions—Mattson has completed more than 500 original, peer-reviewed studies, using something on the order of 20,000 laboratory rodents. He's investigated the progression and prevention of age-related diseases in rats and mice of every kind: black ones and brown ones; agoutis and albinos; juveniles and adults; males and females. Still, he never quite noticed how fat they were—how bloated and sedentary and sickly—until a Tuesday afternoon in February 2007. That's the day it occurred to him, while giving a lecture at Emory University in Atlanta, that his animals were nothing less (and nothing more) than lazy little butterballs. His animals and everyone else's, too.

Using Control Animals Is Problematic

Mattson was lecturing on a research program that he'd been conducting since 1995, on whether a strict diet can help ward off brain damage and disease. He'd generated some dramatic data to back up the theory: If you put a rat on a limited feeding schedule—depriving it of food every other day—and then blocked off one of its cerebral arteries to induce a stroke, its brain damage would be greatly reduced. The same held for mice that had been engineered to develop something like Parkinson's disease: Take away their food, and their brains stayed healthier.

How would these findings apply to humans, asked someone in the audience. Should people skip meals, too? At 5-foot-7 and 125 pounds, Mattson looks like a meal-skipper, and he is one. Instead of having breakfast or lunch, he takes all his food over a period of a few hours each evening—a bowl of steamed cabbage, a bit of salmon, maybe some yogurt. It's not unlike the regime that appears to protect his lab animals from cancer, stroke, and neurodegenerative disease. "Why do we eat three meals a day?" he asks me over the phone, not waiting for an answer. "From my research, it's more like a social thing than something with a basis in our biology."

But Mattson wasn't so quick to prescribe his stern feeding schedule to the crowd in Atlanta. He had faith in his research on diet and the brain but was beginning to realize that it suffered from a major complication. It might well be the case that a mouse can be starved into good health—that a deprived and skinny brain is more robust than one that's well-fed. But there was another way to look at the data. Maybe it's not that limiting a mouse's food intake makes it healthy, he thought; it could be that not limiting a mouse's food makes it sick. Mattson's control animals—the rodents that were supposed to yield a normal response to stroke and Parkinson's—might have been overweight, and that would mean his baseline data were skewed.

"I began to realize that the 'control' animals used for research studies throughout the world are couch potatoes," he tells me. It's been shown that mice living under standard laboratory conditions eat more and grow bigger than their country cousins. At the National Institute on Aging, as at every major research center, the animals are grouped in plastic cages the size of large shoeboxes, topped with a wire lid and a food hopper that's never empty of pellets. This form of husbandry, known as *ad libitum* [at one's pleasure] feeding, is cheap and convenient since animal technicians need only check the hoppers from time to time to make sure they haven't run dry. Without toys or exercise wheels to distract them, the mice are left with nothing to do but eat and sleep—and then eat some more.

That such a lifestyle would make rodents unhealthy, and thus of limited use for research, may seem obvious, but the problem appears to be so flagrant and widespread that few scientists bother to consider it. Ad libitum feeding and lack of exercise are industry-standard for the massive rodent-breeding factories that ship out millions of lab mice and rats every year and fuel a $1.1-billion global business in living reagents for medical research. When Mattson made that point in Atlanta, and suggested that the control animals used in labs were sedentary and overweight as a rule, several in the audience gasped. His implication was clear: The basic tool of biomedicine—and its workhorse in the production of new drugs and other treatments—had been transformed into a shoddy, industrial product. Researchers in the United States and abroad were drawing the bulk of their conclusions about the nature of human disease—and about Nature itself—from an organism that's as divorced from its natural state as feedlot cattle or oven-stuffer chickens. . . .

The Rise of the Factory Mouse

Mattson is not the only one with doubts, nibbling away at the corner of his cage. The rise of the factory mouse has implications that extend far beyond his work on Parkinson's disease and stroke. By focusing so intently on one organism, raised in a certain way, we may be limiting our knowledge of cancer, too, and heart disease, and tuberculosis—the causes of death for many millions of people every year. If Mattson is right, science may be faced with a problem that is mind-boggling in its scope. Funding agencies in the United States and Europe will spend hundreds of millions of dollars in the coming years to further fiddle with and refine the standard organism, dou-

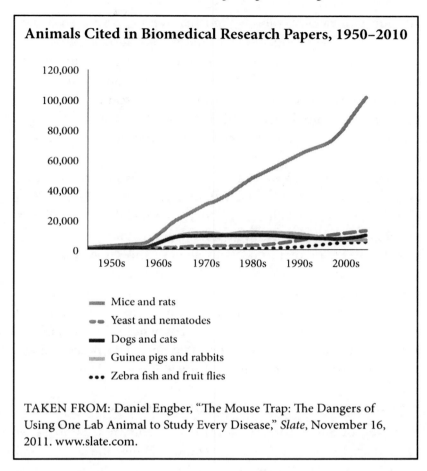

Animals Cited in Biomedical Research Papers, 1950–2010

Legend:
- Mice and rats
- Yeast and nematodes
- Dogs and cats
- Guinea pigs and rabbits
- Zebra fish and fruit flies

TAKEN FROM: Daniel Engber, "The Mouse Trap: The Dangers of Using One Lab Animal to Study Every Disease," *Slate*, November 16, 2011. www.slate.com.

bling down on a bet that goes back at least six decades: Establishing a single animal as the central determinant of how we study human illness, design new medicines, and learn about ourselves.

Just how ubiquitous is the experimental rodent? In the hierarchy of lab animal species, the rat and mouse rule as queen and king. A recent report from the European Union counted up the vertebrates used for experiments in 2008—that's every fish, bird, reptile, amphibian, and mammal that perished in a research setting, pretty much any animal more elaborate than a worm or fly—and found that fish and birds made up 15 percent; guinea pigs, rabbits, and hamsters contributed 5 percent; and horses, monkeys, pigs, and dogs added less than 1 percent. Taken together, lab rats and lab mice accounted for nearly all the rest—four-fifths of the 12 million animals used in total. If you extend those proportions around the world, the use of rodents is astonishing: Scientists are going through some 88 million rats and mice for their experiments and testing every year.

Dead mice pile up more than three times faster than dead rats, which makes sense given their relative size. Cheap, small animals tend to be killed in greater volumes than big ones. A researcher might run through several dozen mice, half a dozen rabbits, or a pair of monkeys to achieve the same result: one published paper. More striking, then, is the extent to which papers about rats and mice—however many animals go into each—dominate the academic literature. According to a recent survey of animal-use trends in neuroscience, almost half the journal pages published between 2000 and 2004 described experiments conducted on rats and mice.

Biomedicine Has Created a Monoculture

A survey of the National Library of Medicine's database of more than 20 million academic citations shows the same trend across the whole of biomedicine. Since 1965, the number of published papers about dogs or cats has remained fairly constant. The same holds true for studies of guinea pigs and rabbits. But over that 44-year stretch, the number of papers involving mice and rats has more than quadrupled. What about the simpler organisms that researchers tend to poke and prod—yeast and zebra fish and fruit flies and roundworms? By 2009, the mouse itself was responsible for three times as many papers as all of those combined.

That is to say, we've arrived at something like a monoculture in biomedicine. The great majority of how we understand disease, and attempt to cure it, derives from a couple of rodents, selected—for reasons that can seem somewhat arbitrary in retrospect—from all the thousands of other mammals, tens of thousands of other vertebrates, and millions of other animal species known to walk or swim or slither the Earth. We've taken the mouse and the rat out of their more natural habitats, from fields and barns and sewers, and refashioned them into the ultimate proxy for ourselves—a creature tailored to, and tailored by, the university basement and the corporate research park.

It's just the latest step in a trend that began more than a century ago. The splendid menagerie that once formed the basis for physiological study—the sheep, the raccoons, the pigeons, the frogs, the birds, the horses—has since the early 1900s been whittled down to a handful of key "model systems": Animals that are special for not being special, that happen to flourish under human care and whose genes we can manipulate most easily; the select and selected group that are supposed to stand in for all creation. Where scientists once tried to assemble knowledge from the splinters of nature, now they erect it from a few standardized parts: An assortment of mammals, some nematodes and fruit flies, E. coli bacteria and Saccharomyces yeast. Even this tiny toolkit of living things has in recent decades been shrunk down to a favored pair, the rat and mouse. The latter in particular has become a biological Swiss army knife—a handyman organism that can fix up data on cancer, diabetes, depression, post-traumatic stress, or any other disease, disorder, or inconvenience that could ever afflict a human being. The modern lab mouse is one of the most glorious products of industrial biomedicine. Yet this powerful tool might have reached the limit of its utility. What if it's taught us all it can?

The Drug Discovery Process
Needs Improvement

The government's top researcher on tuberculosis—still one of the world's most deadly infections—seems to be running a midsized wildlife park out of his Maryland home. In a modest house on a tree-lined street in Germantown, Clif Barry keeps two kinds of turtles, three veiled chameleons, two Jackson's chameleons, six species of frogs, half a dozen fish tanks (filled with cichlids, goldfish, and piranhas, kept separately), two dogs (named Jacques and Gillian), and an Australian tree python. "I'm an animal person," he tells me. "My house would require a zookeeper's license if Montgomery County knew what I had."

Twenty miles away in Bethesda, though, where Barry serves as chief of the Tuberculosis Research Section at the National Institute of Allergy and Infectious Diseases, a single animal has taken over the ecosystem. It has infested every paper and conference, and formed a living, writhing barrier to new drugs on their way to clinical trials. "We've always only tested things in mice," Barry tells me by phone one afternoon. "The truth is that for some questions, mice give you a very nice and easy model system for understanding what's happening in humans, but mice are mice, and people are people. If we look to the mouse to model every aspect of the disease for man, and to model cures, we're just wasting our time."

The problem, he says, begins with the three M's. The process of drug discovery has been carried out in the same way for decades. You start by testing a new compound in a Petri dish, to find out whether it can slow the growth of a particular bacterium in culture. That gives you the smallest dose that has an effect, known as the minimum inhibitory concentration, or "MIC"—the first M. Then you move to a living animal: Does the compound have any effect on the course of disease in a lab mouse? If so, you've cleared the second M, and you're ready to test the compound in the third M, man. Each step leads to the next: No drug can be tested in man until it's been shown to work in mice, and no drug is tested in mice until it's been shown to have a reasonable effect in the dish. "The bad part of that," says Barry, "is that no part of it is predictive:" A new compound that succeeds in the dish might flunk out in the mouse, and something that can cure tuberculosis in a mouse could wash out in people.

Take the example of pyrazinamide, one of the front-line drugs in the treatment of tuberculosis [TB]. Along with three other antibiotics, it forms the cocktail that remains, despite ongoing research, our only way of defeating the infection. But pyrazinamide didn't make it through the three M's: It does nothing in the dish—there's no MIC whatsoever—and it has a weak effect in mice. According to Barry, if a compound like that were discovered in 2011, it would never make its way into clinical trials. Forty years ago, the system wasn't so rigid. A prominent physician and researcher at Britain's Medical Research Council named Wallace Fox saw something intriguing in the animal data: Pyrazinamide's action seemed to persist when those of other drugs had stopped. He insisted on testing the drug in humans, and its effects were profound. The fact that nothing gets to humans today without first passing the mouse test, says Barry, "has cost us a new generation of medicines."

Indeed, there's been no real breakthrough in treating tuberculosis—no major pharmaceutical discoveries—since the early 1970s. The first antibiotic to have any success against the tuberculosis mycobacterium, the first that could penetrate its waxy coating, was discovered (and tested in guinea pigs) in the early 1940s. The best vaccine we have was first used in humans in 1921. (It works pretty well against severe childhood forms of the disease, but less so otherwise.) And the closest thing we have to a miracle cure—the multidrug cocktail that doesn't work against every strain and requires a six-month course of treatment with severe side effects—was finalized during the Nixon administration. Since then, almost every new idea for how to treat TB has come from experiments on lab mice. These have given us enough new data to drown the infected in a tsunami of graphs and tables, to bury them in animal carcasses. Yet we've made little progress—OK, no progress at all—in treating the human disease. Tuberculosis causes more than 2 million deaths every year, and we're using the same medicines we had in 1972.

The Problem with the Mouse Model

One major problem with the mouse model—and the source of its spotty track record in the clinic—is well-known among those in the field: The form of TB that mice happen to get isn't all that much like our own. A human case of the disease begins when infectious bacilli are inhaled into the lungs, where they grow in number as the immune system sends in its soldiers to fight them off. White blood cells swarm the bacteria in a rolling, alveolar scrum, forming a set of pearly-white masses the size of golf balls called granulomas. These are where the war between body and invader plays out in a series of contained skirmishes.

As more immune cells are recruited to fight off the infection, some of the balls swell and stratify into a more developed form: A sphere of macrophages and lymphocytes packed inside a fibrous shell, with a cottage cheese clump of dead cells and bacteria at its core. At this point the battle reaches a stalemate: The bacteria stop dividing; the body has controlled, but not eliminated, the infection. For most people who have the disease, it's a ceasefire that holds indefinitely.

But for some patients a latent case of tuberculosis can suddenly become active. The granulomas rupture and propagate, spilling thousands of organisms into the lungs, where they can be aerosolized, coughed up, and passed on to a new host. Left untreated, the infection migrates into the bloodstream and other organs; widespread inflammation leads to burst arteries or a ruptured esophagus; and in about half of all cases, the patient dies.

The layered granuloma is the defining feature of human tuberculosis: The place where the host fights the infection (successfully or not), and the necessary site of action for any drug. To cure the disease, a treatment must be able to penetrate each ball of cells, whatever its type or composition; every last bacterium must be destroyed. "It's the structure of those granulomas that makes it so difficult to treat TB," says Barry. And they simply don't exist in mice.

If you infect a mouse with TB—if you spritz a puff of infected air into its nostrils through a trumpet, as so many labs do around the world—the animal's lungs quickly fill up with bacteria and immune cells, like a nasty case of pneumonia. There are no discrete balls of tissue, no well-defined granulomas sheathed in fibrin, no array of structures that harbor the bugs at various stages of development. The mice have no special, latent form of TB, either, and no way to pass on the disease. They simply die, after a year or two, of a slow and progressive decline.

That's why we've made so little progress using mice to generate new drugs and treatments, Barry tells me. In the absence of a clear, granulomatous response upon which to model human disease, the second M has become a massive roadblock in the path to a cure. "The vast majority of the money that we spend in clinical trials based on mouse data is completely wasted," he says.

Periodical and Internet Sources Bibliography

The following articles have been selected to supplement the diverse views presented in this chapter.

Terry J. Allen	"Offshoring Human Drug Trials," *In These Times*, April 6, 2010. www.inthesetimes.com.
Michael Brooks	"The Truth About Animal Testing," *New Statesman*, July 26, 2012. www.newstatesman.com.
Andrew Buncombe and Nina Kakhani	"Without Consent: How Drug Companies Exploit Indian 'Guinea Pigs,'" *Independent* (UK), November 14, 2011.
Michelle Chen	"American Science's Racist History Still Haunts the World," *Colorlines*, October 6, 2010. www.colorlines.com.
Donna Dickenson	"Mengele in America," *Project Syndicate*, November 2, 2011. www.project-syndicate.org.
Carl Elliott	"Useless Studies, Real Harm," *New York Times*, July 28, 2011.
Stephanie Kelly	"Testing Drugs on the Developing World," *Atlantic*, February 27, 2013. www.theatlantic.com.
Emily A. Largent, Christine Grady, Franklin G. Miller, and Alan Wertheimer	"Money, Coercion, and Undue Inducement: Attitudes About Payments to Research Participants," *IRB: Ethics & Human Research*, January–February 2012.
Greg McDonald	"Human Guinea Pigs on the Rise as Economy Worsens," *Newsmax*, September 20, 2011. www.newsmax.com.

OPPOSING
VIEWPOINTS®
SERIES

CHAPTER 2

How Should Medical Testing on Humans and Animals Be Regulated?

Chapter Preface

Federal regulations exist for medical testing on both humans and animals. Whereas laws governing the protection of human subjects are codified in numerous separate regulations by several different federal departments and agencies, there is only one federal law that governs the protection of animals used in research.

In 1974 the National Research Act was signed into law, which created the National Commission for the Protection of Human Subjects of Biomedical and Behavioral Research. The commission was charged with identifying the basic ethical principles that should guide biomedical and behavioral research involving human subjects. The outgrowth of the commission's research was the *Belmont Report: Ethical Principles and Guidelines for the Protection of Human Subjects of Research, Report of the National Commission for the Protection of Human Subjects of Biomedical and Behavioral Research*, published in 1979.

Within the *Belmont Report*, the commission identified three basic ethical principles that should guide research involving human subjects: respect for persons, beneficence, and justice. The commission explained that respect for persons requires "that individuals should be treated as autonomous agents" and "that persons with diminished autonomy are entitled to protection." This principle demands that human research subjects are given informed consent for participation in any testing. The second ethical principle of beneficence requires that human subjects be treated in a way that attempts to maximize possible benefits while minimizing possible harms. Thus, the commission notes that risks and benefits must be carefully assessed prior to conducting human subject research. Finally, the commission determined that human subject research must be guided by the ethical principle of justice, ensuring that people are treated equally. Thus, in selecting subjects, care must be taken to ensure that certain groups are not unfairly targeted for greater risks or certain groups targeted for greater benefits.

The *Belmont Report* heavily influenced the adoption of the Federal Policy for the Protection of Human Subjects—or the "Common Rule"—published in 1991 and codified in separate regulations by fifteen federal departments and agencies. The Common Rule explains what research is covered by the regulations and creates guidelines for establishing institutional review boards, or IRBs, which review human subjects research for adherence to the regulations.

The only federal law regulating animal subjects research is the Animal Welfare Act, signed into law in 1966 and enforced by the US Department of Agriculture. The Animal Welfare Act does not apply to research involving all animals, specifically excluding rats of the genus *Rattus* and mice of the genus *Mus*, as well as birds used in research. The act identifies housing and environmental requirements for different species, including cats and dogs, guinea pigs and hamsters, rabbits, nonhuman primates, and marine mammals.

The existing regulations for both human subjects research and animal subjects research are frequently criticized. Yet, there is little agreement even in criticism. Some criticize the regulations for being too stringent and interfering with critical medical research, whereas others charge that humans or animals are not adequately protected by existing regulations.

| "The weaknesses in the oversight system can have consequences that reach beyond the immediate research."

Current Federal Oversight of Human Medical Testing Is Inadequate

Jeanne Lenzer and Shannon Brownlee

In the following viewpoint, Jeanne Lenzer and Shannon Brownlee argue that there are still gaps in the regulatory safety net for human research subjects. They point to a clinical trial that had problems with misinformation of patients, conflicts of interest, and a lack of federal oversight. Lenzer is a medical investigative journalist, and Brownlee is acting director of the Health Policy Program at the New America Foundation and author of Overtreated: Why Too Much Medicine Is Making Us Sicker and Poorer.

As you read, consider the following questions:

1. According to the authors, a 2008 study by the Hastings Center concluded what about human subject safety?

2. What federal government office was created in 2001 to address the medical research oversight system, as stated by the authors?

3. The federal office cited how many medical centers for lapses over the course of nine years, according to Lenzer and Brownlee?

Ten years ago [1999], an 18-year-old student named Jesse Gelsinger died during a medical research trial involving gene therapy at the University of Pennsylvania. The teenager's death, caused by a violent immune reaction to an injection, triggered a federal inquiry, a review of human protection standards in clinical trials and, ultimately, tougher national standards for patient consent.

Now details have surfaced about a clinical trial at Columbia University Medical Center that took place not long after the Gelsinger case, and which raises questions about the regulatory safety net that was the legacy of the teen's death.

Columbia's Trial Is a Cautionary Tale

Federal regulators have cited Columbia for ethical and regulatory mistakes in a clinical trial, completed in 2001, in which more than 200 patients agreed to receive one of four federally approved surgical fluids during open-heart operations. Regulators now have concluded that some patients may have been harmed and have ordered Columbia to track down all participants to inform them of the facts of the study and their surgeries, as the Huffington Post Investigative Fund reported exclusively earlier this month [March 2010]. The hospital has acknowledged flaws in the study but has said there is no evidence those led to the patients' medical problems.

If the Gelsinger case was a pivotal moment in reform, the Columbia case is a cautionary tale, coming to light months after a sobering national review of clinical trials by independent bioethics research institute, the Hastings Center. In its 2008 review, the Hastings Center concluded the human subjects are no better protected today than they were at the time of Gelsinger's death.

The federal order that directed Columbia to find its heart patients and tell them more about their drug study illustrates the continuing weakness in safeguards of clinical trials and specifically the procedures for obtaining informed consent— the written acknowledgement by a patient that he or she understands the risks of participation in a clinical trial.

Collaboration between industry and academic institutions to test drugs and medical devices has increased at such a rate in the past decade that oversight panels are hard pressed to fully review all such trials. The gaps mean that a medical product may receive federal approval and be marketed without regulators or doctors being aware of limitations and biases in its testing history.

In the case of Columbia's study, research that was barred from publication by university officials was nonetheless submitted by the manufacturer to an advisory panel hearing of the U.S. Food and Drug Administration [FDA] as evidence that its product was safer than a competitor's.

Oversight Is Lacking

Vulnerabilities in the oversight system have registered in Washington. The Obama administration recently appointed Jerry Menikoff, a bioethicist and well-known critic of the research oversight process, to head the federal Office of Human Research Protections. That office was created in 2001, within the Department of Health and Human Services, in the wake of Gelsinger's death.

Menikoff, who is also a physician, has argued publicly that patients are often not fully informed or protected when they sign consent forms. "There is good reason to believe that in many thousands of cases, research subjects are not being given the information they most need," Menikoff wrote in "What the Doctor Didn't Say," a book he co-authored in 2006.

"Too much of our current system has contained remnants of a disturbing notion that to have the appropriate amount of research, we need to deceive many patients when they are being asked to participate in clinical trials," Menikoff wrote. All too often, in his view, patients are led to believe they will benefit directly from participating.

An estimated 300,000 studies involving up to 7 million human subjects are conducted each year in the U.S. No government agency or private entity tracks those numbers closely, according to CenterWatch, a Boston-based service that maintains one of the largest databases of clinical trials.

The Impact of Institutional Review Boards

Medical research involving patients is subject to oversight by institutional review boards, or IRBs. There are nearly 4,000 of these boards in the U.S. Most rely on already overscheduled staff at medical centers and research hospitals; some are independent commercial outfits. Each board is responsible for reviewing anywhere from dozens to hundreds of research proposals a year.

Board members are often volunteers with full academic and clinical duties at their hospital or research center. Many describe themselves as hard pressed to keep up with all relevant studies and often rely on the scientific integrity of researchers who propose the clinical trials, according to experts in the medical research field.

"Patient protection is run on an honor system," said Robin Wilson, a law professor at Washington and Lee University. The federal Office of Human Research Protections assumes, unless a complaint is lodged, that hospital boards are vigilant about oversight in clinical trials. The boards, in turn, largely trust researchers to ensure patient safety.

Gaps in Federal Regulations

Not all human research is subject to federal regulations, since the regulations apply only to studies that are federally funded or that involve new drugs and devices for which applications have been filed with the Food and Drug Administration. An estimated 30 percent of studies are not covered. In contrast, each and every experiment involving animals is regulated by the federal government under the Animal Welfare Act.

Paul Gelsinger and Adil E. Shamoo,
"Eight Years After Jesse's Death, Are Human Research
Subjects Any Safer?," Hastings Center Report, *2008.*

Greg Koski, a former head of the Office of Human Research Protections, told the Investigative Fund that he believes it is impossible to know if institutional review boards fully understand the proposed studies and are adequately protecting patients.

"Most IRBs operate behind closed doors . . . in part to protect intellectual property or commercial information," said Koski, an anesthesiologist at Massachusetts General Hospital. Koski now advocates that researchers be trained and certified before they design clinical trials. He also wants to see uniform requirements for all commercial and federally-funded studies and better data collection on the performance of institutional review boards.

The Problem with Clinical Trial Collaborations

In the last nine years, the federal office has cited more than 40 medical centers for lapses ranging from misinforming patients about potential risks to failing to report serious complications.

Some of the cases involved studies that were funded in part by pharmaceutical, biotech and medical device industries. Such collaborations are mutually beneficial. Companies seek out researchers at well-known academic centers who have access to patients willing to participate in trials. Universities find that industry-driven clinical trials enhance their reputations and financial bottom lines.

As collaborations have increased, the clinical trial divisions at many university hospitals have been reorganized in ways that resemble the structures of commercial drug companies, said Jennifer Washburn, author of "University Inc.: The Corporate Corruption of Higher Education." "They now function far more like for-profit research organizations whose purpose is to serve their clients," Washburn said in an interview.

Washburn points out that members of review boards "may be reluctant to interfere or impede the work of their colleagues . . . especially when those colleagues are powerful faculty who bring in substantial revenue into the medical school."

The weaknesses in the oversight system can have consequences that reach beyond the immediate research. If studies are carried out with flaws in design or procedures, the results can affect many more patients than just those who participated in the trial.

In the case of the Columbia trial, Abbott Laboratories contributed $150,000 to the research; a blood expander that Abbott manufactures was one of four used on open-heart patients at the hospital from 1999 to 2001.

Patients signed consent forms but federal regulators have now determined that the patients were unaware of the "true nature" of the study.

Testing the safety of the fluids at high doses was one purpose of the study, Columbia investigators later concluded. The hospital's internal reviews found that the consent form failed to inform patients that hetastarch—a substance used in two of the blood expanders in the study, including the one sold by

Abbott—could prevent blood from clotting properly, especially when used at higher doses. About half of the 215 people in the study were given hetastarch, and some received more than three times the upper limit recommended by the manufacturers, according to documents later filed in court.

After conducting an internal investigation—one of three the hospital would launch about the drug trial—Columbia in 2002 communicated its concerns to federal regulators and barred from publication any scientific findings from the clinical trial.

Questioning the Safety of Blood Expanders

The findings never were published. However, records show, Abbott Laboratories in 2002 provided data from the Columbia study, along with other unpublished studies, to an FDA advisory board deciding what kind of safety labels to put on the Abbott product, Hextend, and that of its main competitor, Hespan, manufactured by B. Braun Medical Inc. Abbott was lobbying the FDA to have its product exempted from a requirement that would require it to contain a warning about bleeding complications during cardiac surgery.

According to FDA records, Abbott used the unpublished studies to raise questions about "excessive bleeding during cardiac surgery" by its competition.

Gary Haynes, chair of the department of anesthesia and critical care at St. Louis University School of Medicine, was among those who provided expert testimony to the FDA panel about commercial blood expanders. Haynes, interviewed for this story, recalls that the unpublished study from Columbia was central to Abbott's argument that its product was safer for heart surgery than its competitor's.

The FDA decided in Abbott's favor, requiring its competitor to include the additional warning about bleeding risks. Abbott's product was sold without the warning about heart surgery.

An Abbott spokesman told the Investigative Fund that the company has no record of how it obtained the data from the Columbia study. The FDA did not respond to questions about the matter.

After the FDA's decision, Abbott paid for full-page advertisements in at least one medical journal, promoting its product for use "even at higher volumes." Hospitals around the country subsequently included the Abbott's blood expander on their list of preferred drugs. The U.S. military, engaged in two wars for much of this decade, names Abbott's Hextend in its Army guide for medical personnel.

Yet the claims that the Abbott product is safer than its competitors have been called into question by subsequent reviews in the medical literature.

In 2003, a published review of 40 studies of intravenous fluids in the journal *Anesthesia & Analgesia* found that virtually all the studies of blood expanders were poorly conducted or reported. The author concluded that the use of blood expanders by anesthesiologists and other physicians was being guided by "dogma and personal beliefs" rather than sound science.

In 2005, another study published in the *Journal of Cardiothoracic and Vascular Anesthesia* found that both Abbott's Hextend, and its competition, Hespan, had the same anti-clotting effect.

A third study, cited in the journal *Chest* in March 2009, had to be halted early because of serious bleeding among heart surgery patients. Those patients were given just one-fifth the average dose of the Abbott drug that patients received in the Columbia study.

> *"Current regulations generally appear to protect people from avoidable harm or unethical treatment, insofar as is feasible given limited resources."*

Current Federal Oversight of Human Medical Testing Could Use Refinement

Presidential Commission for the Study of Bioethical Issues

In the following viewpoint, the Presidential Commission for the Study of Bioethical Issues argues that although the current regulatory environment is basically sound, there are some areas for improvement. In particular, it suggests that more should be done to address research-related injury, create a culture of responsibility among researchers, and implement strategies that help to avoid exploitation of human subjects. The Presidential Commission for the Study of Bioethical Issues is an advisory panel that advises the US president on bioethical issues arising from advances in biomedicine and related areas of science and technology.

Presidential Commission for the Study of Bioethical Issues, "Moral Science: Protecting Participants in Human Subjects Research," December 2011, pp. 2–3, 5–6,–10, 12–13. www.bioethics.gov.

As you read, consider the following questions:

1. According to the commission, the so-called Common Rule generally requires what three standards in human subjects research?

2. The commission claims that previous advisory bodies have made what same recommendation without clear response?

3. The author suggests what strategy for minimizing the potential of exploitation when research is done in low-income communities?

Human research serves to ensure the safety of new medicines, establish tolerable exposure levels for environmental and workplace hazards, and determine the effectiveness of new interventions in public health, education, and countless other fields. Without volunteers, these studies would be impossible to conduct. Recognizing society's responsibility to protect human subjects of research from avoidable harm and unethical treatment, President Barack Obama asked the Presidential Commission for the Study of Bioethical Issues (the Commission) to conduct a thorough review of current regulations and international standards to assess whether they adequately protect human subjects in federally supported scientific studies, no matter where they occur.

Adhering to the Common Rule

The Commission's review confirmed that the federal government supports a diverse and wide-ranging portfolio of research, which includes activities funded directly, or by award or sub-award, throughout the world. Support for medical and public health research predominates, but the federal government also supports a large volume of human subjects research in other fields, including social and behavioral sciences and education.

Sound scientific experimentation is rooted in uncertainty and volunteers cannot be immunized from all physical or psychological risks. However, in order for research with human beings to be ethical, human subjects must be volunteers who give their informed consent, who are treated fairly and respectfully, who are subjected only to reasonable risks from which proportionate humanitarian benefit can be obtained, and who are not treated as mere means to the ends of others. (Some carefully specified and regulated exceptions to informed consent are based on the incapacity of some subjects or the very low risk of the experiments, provided that all the other conditions—including fair and respectful treatment—hold.)

In the absence of these ethical constraints, tragic results may follow. Many prior abuses of human subjects are now carefully documented, and some informed the development of today's federal human subjects protection system. Eighteen federal departments and agencies require adherence to a uniform regulatory floor for human subjects research, known as the "Common Rule," which generally requires informed consent, independent ethical review, and the minimization of avoidable risks. These standards apply to all research funded by these departments and agencies, regardless of where it occurs. The Food and Drug Administration applies essentially the same standards to all research conducted in support of seeking U.S. marketing approval for drugs, devices, and biologics, regardless of the source of funding.

Following the Guiding Ethical Principles

These rules reflect widely accepted principles of ethics. These principles are rooted in longstanding values that find expression in many sources of moral philosophy; theological traditions; and codes, regulations, and rules. They are the bulwark of ethically sound science, or "moral science," as the Commission terms it. Each generation may re-examine how these principles are contextually applied and understood. And, their application or implementation may vary depending on the level of risk that a subject faces. Medical research that poses risk of physical injury rightly raises more concerns than does routine social survey research, for example. Nonetheless, the same ethical principles govern all of these activities, and serve as enduring guideposts that must not be ignored.

The public has a right to expect researchers to abide by rules that satisfy these principles. Researchers themselves benefit from public confidence when they conform to these rules; and with public esteem they earn the ability to conduct potentially important research with public support. Without such earned confidence, research participation may be threatened and critical research jeopardized. More than these measurable effects, society risks irretrievably losing sight of what is inherently owed to fellow human beings and those who deserve special protection by virtue of their willingness to participate in experiments designed to benefit others and advance scientific and social progress.

From time to time society revisits the rules applied to research with human subjects and the implementation of guiding ethical principles. The need for reassessment may arise from challenges presented by novel scientific advances, a perceived mismatch between ethical principles and their implementation, or revelations of abuse. When President Obama charged the Commission with undertaking this review of contemporary human subjects protection standards, he recognized the sacred trust and responsibility that we as a society have to ensure that human research subjects are protected from harm and unethical treatment. . . .

Examining the Current Regulations

The Commission concludes that current regulations generally appear to protect people from avoidable harm or unethical treatment, insofar as is feasible given limited resources, no matter where U.S.-supported research occurs. This conclusion is fully consistent with, and also qualified by, the large yet incomplete set of information made available to the Commission in the time available to carry out its charge. Specifically, the Commission found:

> The current U.S. system provides substantial protections for the health, rights, and welfare of research subjects and, in general, serves to "protect people from harm or unethical treatment" when they volunteer to participate as subjects in scientific studies supported by the federal government. However, because of the currently limited ability of some governmental agencies to identify basic information about all of their human subjects research, the Commission cannot conclude that all federally funded research provides optimal protections against avoidable harms and unethical treatment. The Commission finds significant room for improvement in several areas where, for example, immediate changes can be made to increase accountability and thereby reduce the likelihood of harm or unethical treatment.

In reaching this conclusion, the Commission believes that the ethical principles for human subjects research should not—indeed *must* not—vary depending on the source of funding or location of the research. While the specific methods of implementing the ethical principles of human subjects research are likely to differ, the principles should not. Ethical principles provide the foundation for the rules and regulations that govern human subjects research as well as lay the groundwork upon which everyone who conducts human subjects research must stand.

There is no way to eradicate all risk of harm, particularly in some types of medical and translational research, but the Commission found several important areas where improvement or refinement of the current system is both possible and desirable. . . .

Assessing the Treatment of Research-Related Injury

Those who sponsor or engage in human subjects research have an ethical obligation to protect those who volunteer as research subjects. Almost all other developed nations have instituted policies to require treatment, or compensation for treatment, for injuries suffered by research subjects. The [International Research] Panel advised the Commission to recommend that the United States establish a system to assure compensation for the medical care of human subjects harmed in the course of biomedical research. However, the Commission believes that before altering the current approach to compensation for injuries sustained during federally funded research, the nature and scope of harms that remain unaddressed must be assessed.

Because subjects harmed in the course of human research should not individually bear the costs of care required to treat harms resulting directly from that research, the federal government, through the Office of Science and Technology Policy or the Department of Health and Human Services, should move expeditiously to study the issue of research-related injuries to determine if there is a need for a national system of compensation or treatment for research-related injuries. If so, the Department of Health and Human Services, as the primary funder of biomedical research, should conduct a pilot study to evaluate possible program mechanisms.

The Commission stresses that it is important to recognize the limits of current models for providing compensation, like the National Vaccine Injury Compensation program, and also the various means by which the government may satisfy the ethical obligation to compensate individuals who suffer research-related injuries in a federally funded study. While there are systems already in place for some government research, the Commission recommends a study to evaluate future options and outlines many questions to be considered. It also recognizes that several national bodies have made similar recommendations in the past. Given the seriousness of the ethical concern, and these past efforts, the Commission encourages the government to follow up publicly with its response.

The Commission recognizes that previous presidentially appointed bioethics commissions and other duly appointed advisory bodies have made similar recommendations regarding compensation or treatment for research-related injuries; yet no clear response by the federal government has been issued. Therefore, the federal government, through the Office of Science and Technology Policy or the Department of Health and Human Services, should publicly release reasons for changing or maintaining the status quo.

Creating a Culture of Responsibility

The Commission heard from a wide range of research professionals that the procedural requirements of human subjects regulations are often viewed as unwelcome bureaucratic obstacles to conducting research. The density of some of these requirements can obscure their justification and routinized interpretation can create distance between the underlying ethical principles and how they are viewed and implemented by institutional review boards and the research community. The Commission too recognizes that there is often a fundamental distinction between ethical principles (and the personal responsibilities that must be exercised to effect them), and procedural or policy strategies to apply and implement these principles. While tension between principles and procedures is, in some ways, perennial, the Commission believes that specific steps can be taken now to deflect the tilt that some see favoring process over principle. Two of these recommendations are directed to government specifically, and a third more generally relates to education and the duty to all engaged in the research enterprise.

To promote a better understanding of the context and rationale for applicable regulatory requirements, the Department of Health and Human Services or the Office of Science and Technology Policy should ensure that the ethical underpinnings of regulations are made explicit. This goal is also instrumental to the current effort to enhance protections while reducing burden through reform of the Common Rule and related Food and Drug Administration regulations. Following the principle of regulatory parsimony, regulatory provisions should be rationalized so that fundamental, core ethical standards are clearly articulated.

The Common Rule should be revised to include a section directly addressing the responsibilities of investigators. Doing so would bring it into harmony with the Food and Drug Administration regulations for clinical research and international standards that make the obligations of individual researchers more explicit, and contribute to building a stronger culture of responsibility among investigators.

To ensure the ethical design and conduct of human subjects research, universities, professional societies, licensing bodies, and journals should adopt more effective ways of integrating a lively understanding of personal responsibility into professional research practice. Rigorous courses in bioethics and human subjects research at the undergraduate as well as graduate and professional levels should be developed and expanded to include ongoing engagement and case reviews for investigators at all levels of experience. . . .

Justifying Site Selection

Careful selection of sites for research is important for two sets of reasons. First, the ethical criteria for how subjects must be treated narrows the selection of sites to those that allow for the ethical treatment of subjects. Second, as the *Belmont Report* states, "selection of research subjects needs to be scrutinized in order to determine whether some classes are being systematically selected because of their easy availability, their compromised position, or their manipulability, rather than for reasons directly related to the problem being studied." Thus, careful examination of site selection is extremely important and critical to ensuring that research is done ethically and participants are protected from harm or unethical treatment. Some domestic and international settings present challenges that increase concern about exploitation of human subjects. One proposed strategy for minimizing the potential of exploitation when research is done in low-income communities—whether domestic or international—is to ensure that the proposed study is responsive to the medical, as well as other, needs of the local community or communities. The ethical requirement of responsiveness to local communities needs to be further developed and implemented for responsiveness to become a clearly justified criterion for site selection.

Funders of research should determine that researchers and the sites that they propose to select for their research have the capacity—or can achieve the capacity contemporaneously with the conduct of the research—to support protection of all human subjects.

The federal government, through the Office for Human Research Protections and federal funding agencies, should develop and evaluate justifications and operational criteria for ethical site selection, taking into consideration the extent to which site selection can and should respond to the needs of a broader community or communities. The Office for Human Research Protections should produce, and other agencies should consider developing, guidance for investigators.

> "New sensible guidelines are needed which can be adapted for all types of clinical research, wherever they are done."

Clinical Research: Time for Sensible Global Guidelines

Trudie Lang, Phaik Yeong Cheah, and Nicholas J. White

In the following viewpoint, Trudie Lang, Phaik Yeong Cheah, and Nicholas J. White argue that complex regulations are stifling medical research in developing countries, particularly for non-commercial research. They contend that new evidence-based guidelines are needed. Lang is head of the Global Health Network in the Centre for Clinical Vaccinology and Tropical Medicine at the University of Oxford. Cheah is head of the Clinical Trials Support Group in the Mahidol Oxford Tropical Medicine Research Unit based in Bangkok, Thailand. White is a professor of tropical medicine at the University of Oxford and Mahidol University.

As you read, consider the following questions:

1. According to the authors, what guidelines govern clinical research worldwide?

Trudie Lang, Phaik Yeong Cheah, and Nicholas J. White, "Clinical Research: Time for Sensible Global Guidelines," *The Lancet*, vol. 377, no. 9777, 2011, pp. 1553–1555. Reproduced with permission from Elsevier.

2. What international organization developed guidelines specifically for research in human beings, as stated by the authors?

3. What five examples do the authors give of noncommercial research that could benefit public health?

Clinical research is being slowly strangled by bureaucracy because guidelines that were developed for product-registration trials are being applied rigidly to all types of clinical research.[1,2] Complex, often confusing, and readily misinterpreted regulations, and their consequent spiralling costs, are a dangerous disincentive to medical progress.[2,3] The problem is already serious and is now being exported to the developing world—which can least afford it. Populations in developing countries are under-represented in all areas of clinical research, yet those regions of the world that carry the highest disease burdens obviously stand to gain the most from clinical investigation and improvements in prevention and treatment. This is a time of increased awareness and support for the health problems of developing countries. It is a time of great opportunity for progress. But we are seriously worried that the increasingly complex and expensive standards and regulations—created with the noble intention of protecting patients and ensuring the quality of research and thereby improving health—will not achieve these laudable objectives in the developing world. Indeed they might actually limit research, concentrating it to relatively few wealthy organisations and thereby slowing progress. We need to reverse this trend and aim for a sensible balance. There is a need for new evidence-based guidelines that are appropriate for all types of clinical research. These would be welcomed by researchers everywhere and would be particularly beneficial to research in resource limited settings.

Most regulatory agencies, ethics committees, funders, and medical publishers require that all clinical research accords with the International Conference on Harmonisation's guidelines to Good Clinical Practice (ICH-GCP).[4,5] The basic principles enshrined in the ICH-GCP guidelines are sensible and universally accepted: that researchers should conduct their studies ethically and report accurate and reliable data. However, these guidelines were based on opinion, not evidence, and were written primarily for commercially driven drug-registration studies. ICH-GCP is difficult to interpret for other types of clinical research (panel), such as studies in which the intervention being evaluated is a new approach in nurses' training or treating a patient at home compared with in hospital. Observational, interviewing, or sampling-only studies must all ensure they are working to good clinical practice but investigators find adapting ICH-GCP difficult for these types of clinical research. WHO produced research guidelines[6] that incorporated ICH-GCP and aimed to cover all types of research in human beings. Unfortunately these WHO guidelines are no less cumbersome than the original ICH-GCP guidelines[5] from which they were developed, and because of their rigidity are difficult to implement. Far from enabling, we believe these guidelines have been an impediment to clinical research in developing countries. Unfortunately, any simplified interpretation of ICH-GCP is often met with resistance from those who have been trained to so-called industry standards and regard any other interpretation as inferior.

There are important issues of ownership and responsibility. ICH-GCP was designed as a guideline, and as such is supposed to be interpreted by a study sponsor to fit the specifics of each individual study. In developing countries, much of the experience in clinical trials still comes from externally sponsored drug or vaccine product development trials that are designed, managed, and led by external sponsors who often subcontract the work to privately owned contract-research organisations. These organisations tend to apply the guidelines as a single standard.[7] The perception that the industry ap-

First Five Principles of Good Clinical Research Practice (GCP)

Principle 1: Research involving humans should be scientifically sound and conducted in accordance with basic ethical principles, which have their origin in the Declaration of Helsinki. Three basic ethical principles of equal importance, namely respect for persons, beneficence, and justice, permeate all other GCP principles.

Principle 2: Research involving humans should be scientifically justified and described in a clear, detailed protocol.

Principle 3: Before research involving humans is initiated, foreseeable risks and discomforts and any anticipated benefit(s) for the individual research subject and society should be identified. Research of investigational products or procedures should be supported by adequate non-clinical and, when applicable, clinical information.

Principle 4: Research involving humans should be initiated only if the anticipated benefit(s) for the individual research subject and society clearly outweigh the risks. Although the benefit of the results of the trial to science and society should be taken into account, the most important considerations are those related to the rights, safety, and well-being of the research subjects.

Principle 5: Research involving humans should receive independent ethics committee/institutional review board (IEC/IRB) approval/favourable opinion prior to initiation.

World Health Organization, "WHO Principles of GCP," Handbook for Good Clinical Research Practice, *2005.* www.who.int.

proach is necessary could discourage investigators from planning and running their own trials to answer local disease-management issues, because they perceive that full application of ICH-GCP is an unaffordable and unachievable gold-standard (and anything less is considered of lower value). Ethical, valid, and credible clinical research outside the regulatory pathway does not need to be complicated or expensive. Simplified common-sense good practices that preserve the essential elements of obtaining valid data with high ethical standards are compatible with pragmatic and flexible study-specific application of ICH-GCP. However, having the skills and experience to adapt ICH-GCP, and having the confidence and mandate to do so, is uncommon in developing countries. Researchers from all regions would benefit from pragmatic new good-practice guidelines to enable and encourage this goal.

Globally there is a recognition that things have gone too far.[8-12] Running clinical research studies has become too difficult and too expensive and, as a result, less non-commercial research is being started.[8] Increasingly prescriptive requirements for full ICH-GCP are an important contributor to a dangerous decline in clinical investigation.[3] To make improvements to public health, more disease-management studies are needed to evaluate available and affordable interventions. Examples include: dose-optimisation studies (many drugs widely used in developing countries are prescribed in the wrong doses, particularly in young children and pregnant women); drug interaction assessments; new indication evaluations; cost-effectiveness studies; and management protocol evaluations. Clinical physiology investigations are also difficult under current guidelines. Finding a pragmatic balance between responsible conduct and adequate documentation should be possible, and would facilitate relevant research and health improvement.[9-12] New sensible guidelines are needed which can be adapted for all types of clinical research, wherever they are done. We suggest that WHO's current guidelines for good clinical practice should be revised in this light. Development of new guidelines appropriate for all types of clinical research will facilitate medical progress and therefore improve global health.

Notes

1. McMahon AD, Conway DI, Macdonald TM, McInnes GT. The unintended consequences of clinical trials regulations. *PLoSMed* 2009; 3:e1000131.
2. Editorial. Faltering cancer trials. *New York Times* April 24, 2010. http://www.newyorktimes.com/2010/04/25/opinion/25sun1.html (accessed Dec 6, 2010).
3. Yusuf S, Bosch J, Devereaux P, et al. Sensible guidelines for the conduct of large randomized trials. *Clin Trials* 2008; 5:238–39.
4. DeAngelis C, Drazen JM, Frizelle FA, et al. Clinical trial registration: a statement from the International Committee of Medical Journal Editors. *Lancet* 2004; 364:911–12.
5. International Conference on Harmonisation of Technical Requirements for Registration of Pharmaceuticals for Human Use. Guideline for Good Clinical Practice 1996; E6(R1). http://www.ich.org/fileadmin/Public_Web_Site/ICH_Products/Guidelines/Efficacy/E6_R1/Step4/E6_R1__Guideline.pdf (Accessed Feb 8, 2011.)
6. WHO. Handbook for good clinical research practice (GCP): guidance for implementation. 2005. http://apps.who.int/medicinedocs/documents/s14084e/s14084e.pdf (accessed Dec 6, 2010).
7. Shuchman M. Commercializing clinical trials—risks and benefits of the CRO boom. *N Engl J Med* 2007; 357:1365–68.
8. Morice AH. The death of academic clinical trials. *Lancet* 2003; 361:1568.
9. Hemmincki A, Kellokumpu-Lehtinen PL. Harmful impact of EU clinical trials directive. *BMJ* 2006; 332:501–02.

10. White NJ. Clinical trials in tropical diseases: a politically incorrect view. *Trop Med Int Health* 2006; 11:1483–84.

11. Bosch X. Europe's restrictive rules strangling clinical research. *Nat Med* 2005; 11:1260.

12. Grimes DA, Hubacher D, Nanda K, Schulz KF, Moher D, Altman DG. The Good Clinical Practice guideline: a bronze standard for clinical research. *Lancet* 2005; 366:172 –74.

> *"The majority of animal experiments do not contribute to improving human health, and the value of the role that animal experimentation plays in most medical advances is questionable."*

Medical Testing on Animals Is Cruel and Unnecessary

People for the Ethical Treatment of Animals (PETA)

In the following viewpoint, People for the Ethical Treatment of Animals (PETA) argues that animal experimentation does not advance human health because of the important differences between animals and humans. PETA contends that animals used in experiments are inadequately protected from suffering and many animals are not protected at all by the law. PETA concludes that new models for advancing medicine need to be developed that do not depend upon experimentation on animals. PETA is an animal rights organization.

As you read, consider the following questions:

1. According to PETA, a poll found that what percent of adults oppose the use of animals in scientific research?

2. PETA claims that one of the largest sources of funding for animal experimentation comes from what publicly funded government agencies?

3. There are how many US Department of Agriculture (USDA) inspectors for the nine thousand facilities the USDA regulates, according to the author?

Each year, more than 100 million animals—including mice, rats, frogs, dogs, cats, rabbits, hamsters, guinea pigs, monkeys, fish, and birds—are killed in U.S. laboratories for chemical, drug, food, and cosmetics testing; biology lessons; medical training; and curiosity-driven experimentation. Before their deaths, some are forced to inhale toxic fumes, others are immobilized in restraint devices for hours, some have holes drilled into their skulls, and others have their skin burned off or their spinal cords crushed. In addition to the torment of the actual experiments, animals in laboratories are deprived of everything that is natural and important to them—they are confined to barren cages, socially isolated, and psychologically traumatized. The thinking, feeling animals who are used in experiments are treated like nothing more than disposable laboratory equipment.

Animal Experiments Do Not Improve Human Health

While a Pew Research poll found 43 percent of adults surveyed oppose the use of animals in scientific research, other surveys suggest that those who do accept animal experimentation do so only because they believe it to be necessary for medical progress. The reality is that the majority of animal experiments do not contribute to improving human health, and the value of the role that animal experimentation plays in most medical advances is questionable.

In an article published in *The Journal of the American Medical Association*, researchers [Daniel G. Hackam and

© Mike Flanagan/www.CartoonStock.com.

Donald A. Redelmeier] warned that "patients and physicians should remain cautious about extrapolating the finding of prominent animal research to the care of human disease . . . poor replication of even high-quality animal studies should be expected by those who conduct clinical research."

Diseases that are artificially induced in animals in a laboratory are never identical to those that occur naturally in human beings. And because animal species differ from one another biologically in many significant ways, it becomes even more unlikely that animal experiments will yield results that will be correctly interpreted and applied to the human condition in a meaningful way.

For example, according to former National Cancer Institute Director Dr. Richard Klausner, "We have cured mice of cancer for decades, and it simply didn't work in humans." And although at least 85 HIV/AIDS vaccines have been successful in nonhuman primate studies, as of 2010, every one of nearly 200 preventive and therapeutic vaccine trials has failed to demonstrate benefit to humans. In one case, an AIDS vaccine that was shown to be effective in monkeys failed in human clinical trials because it did not prevent people from developing AIDS, and some believe that it made them *more* susceptible to the disease. According to a report [by Steve Connor and Chris Green] in the British newspaper *The Independent*, one conclusion from the failed study was that "testing HIV vaccines on monkeys before they are used on humans, does not in fact work."

Ninety-two percent of drugs—those that have been tested on animals and *in vitro*—do not make it through Phase 1 of human clinical trials (the initial studies that determine reaction, effectiveness, and side effects of doses of a potential drug).

In addition, the results of animal experiments can be variable and easily manipulated. Research published in the journal *Annals of Internal Medicine* [by Steve Woloshin et al.] revealed that universities commonly exaggerate findings from animal experiments conducted in their laboratories and "often promote research that has uncertain relevance to human health and do not provide key facts or acknowledge important limitations." One study of media coverage of scientific meetings [by Steven Woloshin and Lisa Schwartz] concluded that news stories often omit crucial information and that "the public may be misled about the validity and relevance of the science presented." Because experimenters rarely publish results of failed animal studies, other scientists and the public do not have ready access to information on the ineffectiveness of animal experimentation.

The Public Is Funding Animal Experimentation

Through their taxes, charitable donations, and purchases of lottery tickets and consumer products, members of the public are ultimately the ones who—knowingly or unknowingly—fund animal experimentation. One of the largest sources of funding comes from publicly funded government granting agencies such as the U.S. National Institutes of Health (NIH). Approximately 47 percent of NIH-funded research involves experimentation on nonhuman animals, and in 2009, the NIH budgeted nearly $29 billion for research and development. In addition, many charities—including the March of Dimes, the American Cancer Society, and countless others—use donations to fund experiments on animals. One-third of the projects funded by the National Multiple Sclerosis Society involve animal experimentation.

Despite the vast amount of public funds being used to underwrite animal experimentation, it is nearly impossible for the public to obtain current and complete information regarding the animal experiments that are being carried out in their communities or funded with their tax dollars. State open-records laws and the U.S. Freedom of Information Act can be used to obtain documents and information from state institutions, government agencies, and other federally funded facilities, but private companies, contract labs, and animal breeders are exempt. In many cases, institutions that are subject to open-records laws fight vigorously to withhold information about animal experimentation from the public.

There Is a Lack of Regulation

Despite the countless animals killed each year in laboratories worldwide, most countries have grossly inadequate regulatory measures in place to protect animals from suffering and distress or to prevent them from being used when a non-animal approach is readily available. In the U.S., the most commonly used species in laboratory experiments (mice, rats, birds, reptiles, and amphibians) are specifically exempted from even the minimal protections of the federal Animal Welfare Act (AWA). Laboratories that use only these species are not required by law to provide animals with pain relief or veterinary care, to search for and consider alternatives to animal use, to have an institutional committee review proposed experiments, or to be inspected by the U.S. Department of Agriculture (USDA) or any other entity. Experimenters don't even have to count the mice and rats they kill. Some estimates indicate that as many as 800 U.S. laboratories are not subject to federal laws and inspections because they experiment exclusively on mice, rats, and other animals whose use is unregulated.

As for the approximately 9,000 facilities that the USDA does regulate (of which about 1,000 are designated for "research"), only 99 USDA inspectors are employed to oversee their operations. Reports over a span of 10 years concluded that even the minimal standards set forth by the AWA are not being met by these facilities. In 2000, a USDA survey of the agency's laboratory inspectors revealed serious problems in numerous areas, including "the search for alternatives [and] review of painful procedures." A September 2005 audit report issued by the USDA Office of the Inspector General (OIG) found ongoing "problems with the search for alternative research, veterinary care, review of painful procedures, and the researchers' use of animals." The OIG report estimated that experimenters failed to search for alternatives at almost one-third of facilities.

Even animals who are covered by the law can be burned, shocked, poisoned, isolated, starved, forcibly restrained, addicted to drugs, and brain-damaged—no procedures or experiments, regardless of how trivial or painful they may be, are prohibited by law. When valid non-animal research methods are available, no law requires experimenters to use such methods instead of animals.

Fighting Animal Experimentation

Human clinical, population, and *in vitro* studies are critical to the advancement of medicine; even animal experimenters need them—if only to confirm or reject the validity of their experiments. However, research with human participants and other non-animal methods does require a different outlook, one that is creative and compassionate and embraces the underlying philosophy of ethical science. Animal experimenters artificially induce diseases; clinical investigators study people who are already ill or who have died. Animal experimenters want a disposable "research subject" who can be manipulated as desired and killed when convenient; clinicians must do no harm to their patients or study participants. Animal experimenters face the ultimate dilemma—knowing that their artificially created "animal model" can never fully reflect the human condition, while clinical investigators know that the results of their work are directly relevant to people.

Human health and well-being can also be promoted by adopting nonviolent methods of scientific investigation and concentrating on the prevention of disease before it occurs, through lifestyle modification and the prevention of further environmental pollution and degradation. The public needs to become more aware and more vocal about the cruelty and inadequacy of the current research system and must demand that its tax dollars and charitable donations not be used to fund experiments on animals.

"The use of animals is but one link in the research chain, but it is a vital link."

Medical Research Involving Animals Is Humane and Necessary

Americans for Medical Progress

In the following viewpoint, Americans for Medical Progress argues that biomedical research using animals is critical for advancing the ability to prevent, diagnose, and treat disease in people and animals. Americans for Medical Progress contends that animals used in research are protected by laws and guidelines and cared for by highly trained professionals who work to minimize discomfort. Americans for Medical Progress is an organization that aims to protect society's investment in research by developing public understanding of and support for the humane, necessary, and valuable use of animals in medicine.

As you read, consider the following questions:

1. According to Americans for Medical Progress, humans share what percent of their DNA with chimpanzees?

2. Rodents and fish comprise what percent of all animals used in research, according to Americans for Medical Progress?

3. According to Americans for Medical Progress, what percent of animals used in research are bred specifically for research purposes?

Each species in the animal kingdom is unique. But just as there are differences, there are also key similarities. This is what comparative medicine is about: researchers use both similarities and differences to gain insight into the many complex human biological systems.

Researchers often work with animal models that have biological systems similar to that of a human. For instance, swine and humans share similar cardiovascular and skin systems. By working with swine, researchers are better able to develop and study new heart medicines and treatments for skin diseases.

To study genetic disorders such as Down Syndrome or Parkinson's Disease, researchers might study a mouse model which shares 94% of its DNA with humans. Organisms that look very different can be very similar genetically. Chimpanzees share 98.7% of their DNA with humans. Zebrafish share 75–80% of their DNA with humans. Bananas share 50%.

The differences exhibited in a research model can also provide great insights. For instance, sharks rarely get cancer, cockroaches can regenerate damaged nerves, and some amphibians can regrow lost limbs. By studying these animals we may learn how they accomplish these remarkable feats and apply the principles to human medicine.

Who Cares for Animals in Research?

One of the most important, but unknown facts about biomedical research is that just like at your pet's veterinarian's office, there are research veterinarians, husbandry specialists and animal health technicians—people who care deeply for animals—ensuring that animals in research receive the highest quality of care. These well-trained professionals work directly with researchers to minimize discomfort or distress, two factors that affect the well-being of animals as well as the quality of the data collected in the study.

Most research animals do not experience procedures that are any more invasive than what most people face during an annual physical examination. When potentially uncomfortable procedures are involved, anesthetics and analgesics are used to relieve discomfort.

Regulatory laws and guidelines, such as those listed in the U.S. Animal Welfare Act (AWA), which excludes rats, mice and birds, and in the Public Health Service (PHS) Policy, which covers all vertebrate animals in federally-funded research, mandate high-quality nutrition, housing and veterinary care for research animals.

Research institutions are required to have an Institutional Animal Care and Use Committee (IACUC). IACUCs approve and review research protocols, ensure that anesthesia and postoperative medications are used when appropriate, and that alternatives to animals are sought out and integrated into studies whenever possible.

Most institutions go above and beyond regulatory requirements by volunteering to have their programs reviewed every three years by the Association for Assessment and Accreditation of Laboratory Animal Care International (AAALAC). This accreditation process is very stringent and institutions with AAALAC accreditation are known for their commitment to excellence and humane animal care....

Laboratory animal science professionals know that animal-based research leads to treatments and cures for both people and animals. By caring for animals in research, they provide hope for you and your loved ones, including your pets, and they feel very passionate about their work....

Examining Methods Used in Animal Research

Most research questions can only be answered by harvesting the organ or tissue of interest and examining it at the microscopic and molecular level and animals must be euthanized for this reason. The American Veterinary Medical Association (AVMA) Guidelines on Euthanasia ensure that euthanasia is performed as humanely as possible. Several research institutions have adoption programs for animals in studies that do not require euthanasia. . . .

It's estimated that rodents and fish comprise well over 95% of all animals used in research. The numbers of mice and zebrafish have increased due to the ongoing development of genetic research tools. These methods allow researchers to modify the genome in animals to model common diseases in order to study potential cures. For example, scientists have been able to insert the human genes responsible for a type of Alzheimer's disease into rodents, resulting in the rodents' developing the cognitive dysfunction and memory loss that people experience. . . .

Research Animals Are Necessary

In many cases [computers have replaced research animals], but while computers provide terrific resources for researchers all over the world, they do have limitations. For instance, computers are only able to provide information or models of known "phenomena." Because research consistently seeks answers to unknowns, a computer is unable to simulate how a particular cell might interact or react with a medical compound, or how a complex biological system such as the circulatory system will react to a new drug directed to improve organ function.

A single living cell is many times more complex than even the most sophisticated computer program. There are an estimated 50–100 *trillion* cells in the human body, all of which communicate and interact using a complicated biochemical language—a language researchers have only just begun to learn. Studies using isolated cells or tissues almost always precede animal-based research, but researchers must study whole living systems to understand the effectiveness of treatments, and their potential benefits and dangers.

Federal law requires that all new drugs, medical devices and procedures first be evaluated in animals for safety and efficacy before clinical (human) trials can begin. . . .

Researchers Have a Moral Obligation to Laboratory Animals

As living beings with a conscience, we cannot ignore either human or animal discomfort. Laboratory animal care professionals provide research animals with clean and enriched environments, proper nutrition, and specialized veterinary care, to minimize distress and discomfort.

Not only humans, but also animals—pets, livestock and wildlife—benefit from animal-based research. Almost every discovery (antibiotics, anesthetics, surgical techniques, imaging modalities, etc.) developed through studies with animals also has a positive effect on veterinary medicine.

Researchers have a moral obligation to use all tools available to enhance our ability to prevent, diagnose, and treat disease in people and animals. The use of animals in medical research is not the only resource available: computers, molecular models, in-vitro tissue cultures, epidemiology, and other processes are all part of the quest for treatments and cures. The use of animals is but one link in the research chain, but it is a vital link. . . .

Doctors, scientists and laboratory animal care professionals are involved in research because they recognize the limitations in our current ability to prevent, diagnose, and cure disease in humans and animals. Biomedical research is a noble profession. Many in the field could make more money following other career paths.

Animal-based research is *extremely* expensive and it requires a tremendous investment in well-trained people and special facilities. It is also heavily regulated: an institution must spend a significant amount of time and money to ensure that all applicable regulations and guidelines are met. Conducting animal-based research is not something that institutions undertake without a great deal of deliberation and preparation. . . .

Defining the Term "Cruelty Free"

The law requires that all new chemical compounds be screened for safety using a living system.

It is important to understand what "cruelty free" labels really mean. By definition anyone can use "cruelty free" labels if:

1. as the distributing manufacturer they have not directly evaluated the product in animals. *A company can still use the "cruelty-free" label if they send their product to another company for screening in animals.*

2. some (but not all) components of the product have been screened with animals. *In some cases, products that have been previously evaluated and found safe may be used by other companies and marketed as "cruelty free." For example, if compound A was safe for animals and compound B was also safe, companies can combine compound A and B into compound C and, without further screening with animals, sell it labeled as "cruelty free" and "not tested on animals."* . . .

Most Laboratory Animals Are Bred for Research

Over 99% of the animals used in today's research are "purpose bred" (i.e., bred specifically for research purposes). Those not specifically created for research come from licensed Class B animal dealers that are regulated and inspected by the USDA

[US Department of Agriculture]. Pets do become lost and may never be found but that does not mean that they end up in research laboratories. Pet owners have a responsibility to make sure their animals can be easily identified and returned if lost—through collars with tags, tattoos and/or microchips.

Periodical and Internet Sources Bibliography

The following articles have been selected to supplement the diverse views presented in this chapter.

Michael Brooks	"The Truth About Animal Testing," *New Statesman*, July 26, 2012. www.newstatesman.com.
Kathleen M. Conlee and Andrew N. Rowan	"The Case for Phasing Out Experiments on Primates," *Hastings Center Report*, November–December 2012. www.thehastingscenter.org.
Carl Elliott	"The Deadly Corruption of Clinical Trials," *Mother Jones*, September–October 2010.
Daniel Engber	"Septic Shock," *Slate*, February 13, 2013. www.slate.com.
R. Karl Hanson et al.	"Incentives for Offender Research Participation Are Both Ethical and Practical," *Criminal Justice and Behavior*, November 2012.
Peter H. Kahn, Jr.	"Is Animal Research Acceptable?," *Psychology Today*, February 23, 2011. www.psychologytoday.com.
People's World	"The Horror in Guatemala," September 2, 2011. www.pww.org.
Harriet A. Washington	"Bad Medicine," *New Scientist*, January 21, 2012.
Walter E. Williams	"Invisible Victims," *Townhall*, October 13, 2010. www.townhall.com.
Joanne Zurlo	"No Animals Harmed: Toward a Paradigm Shift in Toxicity Testing," *Hastings Center Report*, November–December 2012. www.thehastingscenter.org.

OPPOSING VIEWPOINTS® SERIES

CHAPTER 3

What Are Some Concerns About Diagnostic Medical Tests?

Chapter Preface

Diagnostic medical tests are a central part of effective health care, allowing doctors to effectively identify and treat disease correctly. However, with the growth in the number of diagnostic medical tests comes a growth in the cost. A 2012 report by the Institute of Medicine estimates that in 2009, the United States spent about $210 billon on unnecessary medical services, including medical testing. The unnecessary costs are paid by government and by insurance companies, resulting in higher taxes and higher insurance premiums for individuals and businesses. Consequently, all Americans have a vested interest in ensuring that diagnostic medical tests are not overused.

The American Board of Internal Medicine Foundation and the National Physicians Alliance recently launched the Choosing Wisely campaign in order to promote conversations between physicians and patients that help patients choose care that is supported by evidence, not duplicative, free from harm, and truly necessary. In conjunction with US specialty societies representing more than five hundred thousand physicians, they developed lists of *Five Things Physicians and Patients Should Question* for each specialty society in recognition of the importance of physician and patient conversations to improve care and eliminate unnecessary tests and procedures.

Among the many suggestions on the lists were several proposals for ending unnecessary medical testing. One suggestion for the American College of Physicians was, "Don't obtain imaging studies in patients with non-specific low back pain." They cautioned that back pain that is not attributed to a specific disease or spinal abnormality usually subsides within a month, with or without testing. Imaging tests by computed tomography (CT) scan cost about $340 and by magnetic resonance imaging (MRI) scan cost about $660. Besides the cost, they note that the testing can expose the patient to radiation when performed on certain areas and, as such, the testing may not only fail to benefit the patient, but also could end up causing harm.

Recommendations to avoid certain medical tests because of cost and possible ineffectiveness seem reasonable. However, when the individual that might be helped is oneself or a loved one, issues of cost and possible ineffectiveness are less likely to be compelling in the absence of significant risk, especially if health insurance will cover the cost. In a small number of cases, lower back pain will be the result of a tumor that could be found through testing. Thus, although some blanket generalizations can be made about medical testing, they are not always compelling when faced with an individual situation.

> *"Billions of health-care dollars may have been misspent on mammograms for women under 50 . . . that were either unnecessary, or which caused women needless psychic and physical trauma."*

Evidence Fails to Support Routine Mammograms Starting at Age Forty

John Crewdson

In the following viewpoint, John Crewdson argues that confusion about a recent government-sponsored task force's recommendation that women not start routine screening mammograms until age fifty is due to a misinterpretation of statistics and confusing coverage of the issue by the news media. Crewdson claims that scientific research supports the recommendation that routine mammogram screening for women in their forties has little benefit and the potential for harm. Crewdson is a senior investigator with the Project on Government Oversight.

As you read, consider the following questions:

1. According to Crewdson, in 2002 an update by Swedish researchers on five of six Swedish trials concluded that there was virtually no benefit from mammograms for women under what age?

2. The author claims that the Swedish researchers found that the death rate from breast cancer among women who received mammograms was 0.4 percent whereas the rate for women without mammograms was what?

3. Crewdson faults what three entities with women being ill-informed about breast cancer?

In January 2002, Umea, Sweden was about the coldest inhabited place on earth. But it was at Umea University, in an office festooned with Sweden's ubiquitous winter candles, that Lennarth Nystrom was carrying out his critical research: analyzing and updating the half-dozen Swedish mammography studies that tell us nearly all of what we know about the value of that procedure.

Swedish Research on Mammograms

Sweden is the birthplace of mammography, and the Swedish mammography trials, which have monitored some 265,000 women in Malmo, Stockholm, Goteborg and other Swedish cities for nearly 30 years, are accepted by physicians and researchers worldwide as the most authoritative.

When I visited Nystrom that frigid winter, he and several distinguished Swedish colleagues were preparing to publish a periodic update of five of the six major Swedish trials.

Their conclusion, which the update itself called "surprising": there was "virtually no" benefit from mammograms for women under 55.

That was more than seven years ago.

A New Government Recommendation Causes Controversy

Much of the confusion and controversy spawned by this week's report [November 2009], by a government-sponsored task force, that screening mammograms are not helpful and may be harmful for women under age 50, has to do with the apparent suddenness of the decision, reversing a quarter-century of advice to begin annual screening at age 40.

But while the report is new, the underlying data has been available since March of 2002, when *The Lancet*, a widely respected British medical journal, published the Swedish update, known as a meta-analysis—a statistical procedure in which the results of the five independent trials were added together to mimic one gargantuan trial.

Although I wrote about the update on the front page of the *Chicago Tribune*, I was the only American reporter at the accompanying Stockholm news conference. The American Cancer Society, and the American College of Radiology, whose members make their living reading mammograms, continued to urge women to begin annual mammograms at age 40.

Now that the task force has changed its recommendation, it seems possible that billions of health-care dollars may have been misspent on mammograms for women under 50—or, according to the Swedish update, under 55—that were either unnecessary, or which caused women needless psychic and physical trauma.

Granted, biostatistics are not easy to understand, and harder to explain to a lay audience. But the current controversy over the task force's report owes much to the media's confusing coverage, some of which has been misinformed, including by TV doctors who ought to know better.

Exaggerating the Advantages of Screening

The confusion has been abetted by the American Cancer Society [ACS], whose position appeared to have softened, then hardened again, in recent weeks.

Last month, Dr. Otis Brawley, the cancer society's chief medical officer, was quoted in the *New York Times* admitting "that American medicine has overpromised when it comes to screening. The advantages to screening have been exaggerated."

Another *Times* article quoted Dr. Susan Love, a leading breast surgeon, calling the under-50 question "the third rail" and praising Brawley for questioning the status quo.

"I really don't think we should be routinely screening women under 50," Love told the *Times*. "There's no data showing it works."

I wasn't surprised by Brawley's statement, since he had expressed the same view to me when we met at a cancer symposium in Milan in 2003. Following the task force report's release, however, Brawley appeared to change direction, telling *The Times* that the cancer society had concluded that the benefits of annual mammograms beginning at 40 "outweighed the risks" and that the ACS was sticking by its earlier advice.

"He's trying to save his job," one of Brawley's colleagues said. "He was broiled at home for the interview in which he said that we (the medical establishment) are 'overselling' screening."

Interpreting the Statistics

In his recent comments, the ACS's Brawley has repeated that regular screening mammograms reduce the incidence of breast cancer in women age 40 to 50 by 15 percent—the same finding as the seven-year-old Swedish update. It should be noted that *before* the update, mammography advocates had been claiming that regular mammograms could reduce the risk of dying from breast cancer by a whopping 30 percent. The update knocked that number down, putting the benefit for women age 40 to 74 at 20 percent, a number *The Lancet* described as "modest," and for women 40–49 at 15 percent.

Thirty percent, 20 percent, and even 15 percent sound like large numbers. Women can be forgiven for asking why a procedure that offers a 15 or 20 percent better chance of surviving breast cancer should be put on the shelf. But even the 15 percent figure is in question.

Dr. Donald Berry, head of biostatistics at the M.D. Anderson Cancer Center in Houston, points out that if the Swedish update is read carefully, the benefit for women 40–50 is really only 9 percent, which is not statistically significant—meaning it could represent the play of chance and not a real advantage.

What Brawley and other mammography advocates flashing across TV screens lately have failed to mention is that the numbers they are flinging around are the *relative* benefit. Utterly obscured is the number that really matters, the *absolute* benefit (Brawley did not respond to an email requesting comment).

The Impact of Mammograms

Once the difference is understood, it's much easier to see how little advantage is derived from screening mammograms. For example, the relative survival benefit of 20 percent among women 40–74 who had mammograms in the Swedish trials translates to 511 women dead of breast cancer out of 130,000 who were screened for 15 years—a death rate of 0.4 percent.

Among the comparison group of 117,000 Swedish women who did not have mammograms, the breast cancer death count was 585 women, or 0.5 percent. True, that's a 20 percent relative benefit in favor of mammography. But 0.4 and 0.5 are very tiny numbers.

M.D. Anderson's Berry, who co-authored a companion paper to the task force report, calculates that a decade of mammograms in a woman's 40s increases her lifespan by an average of 5 days.

"The estimated average of 5 days of life lost if a woman in her early forties delays mammography for 10 years is similar to that for riding a bicycle for 15 hours without a helmet (or 50 hours if wearing a helmet)," Berry says, or of "gaining two ounces of body weight (and keeping them on)." (The only lifestyle feature that appears to correlate with breast cancer risk is obesity.)

Given the intensive, virtually nationwide breast cancer screening underway in Sweden, one would expect that country's breast cancer death rate to have fallen precipitously over the past two decades. But between 1990—the year regular mammograms became available to nearly all Swedish women—and 1998, Sweden's national breast cancer death rate fell by a scant 2 percent, or less than one fewer death in every 100,000 women.

The Downside of Mammograms

Largely due to the publicity campaigns surrounding "early detection" for breast cancer, there is an inclination to see mammography as a lifesaving procedure with no downside. And women whose breast cancers were found via a mammogram and lived to tell the story are often convinced the mammogram saved their lives.

Such thinking is understandable. But breast tumors, not fatal by themselves, can metastasize to the lungs or other vital organs *before* they are large enough to be discovered by a mammogram—in which case the women is likely to die whether she has a mammogram or not.

Also frequently overlooked is the fact that mammograms pick up not only malignant tumors but all manner of benign cysts, masses and other anomalies that must then be investigated. The results of such findings can be both traumatic and costly.

Another *Lancet* study concluded that for every 10,000 mammograms given to apparently healthy women, doctors will order an average of 647 "diagnostic" mammograms, which are more painstaking and expensive, to re-examine something that appeared suspicious the first time around.

Determining which of those women have cancer, *The Lancet* said, also will require 358 breast examinations by ultrasound; 313 biopsies, including 209 in which part of the breast containing the abnormality is surgically removed, and 500 additional doctor's office visits.

The decision health insurers—and federal legislators—must now face is whether spending billions of dollars each year on mammograms and their subsequent procedures is the best use of scarce resources, or if those billions should be spent in some other way that could prevent even more deaths, such as intensive nationwide smoking cessation programs that would attack the major cancer killer among women.

The Media Relies on Anecdotal Cases

The task force report also ignited a flap with its recommendation that, after years of being exhorted to examine their breasts monthly in the shower, women can now forget about self-exams. In response we have heard from women who discovered their breast tumors in the shower and lived to join the ranks of breast cancer survivors. And it's true that most breast tumors are discovered by women themselves, rather than by mammograms.

But as with mammography, discovering a breast tumor with a self-exam is no guarantee that the patient will live to tell about it. Rather than looking at anecdotal cases, the benefits of self-exams are best understood by observing large and statistically significant populations of women. In 2002, the same year the Swedish update was published, the final results were made available from a huge and careful trial involving more than 260,000 female Shanghai factory workers—a near-perfect homogenous and regimented environment in which to conduct such a study.

Half the women, chosen at random, were taught by trained nurses to do breast self-exams. The other half were not. After more than a decade, there was no difference in cancer mortality between the groups.

So much for breast self-examination. But doctors and nurses either ignored the Chinese study or, more likely, were unaware of it. As a result, more seven-year-old data is now being passed off as a sudden paradigm shift.

There are multiple reasons women are ill-informed about breast cancer. The fault lies primarily with their physicians, the cancer establishment, and the news media—especially the news media. Until coverage of breast cancer rises above the level of scary warnings mixed with heartwarming stories of cancer survivors, women are likely to go on being perplexed.

| *"Women age 40 and older should have*
| *mammograms every 1 to 2 years."*

Women Should Receive Screening Mammograms Starting at Age Forty

National Cancer Institute

In the following viewpoint, the National Cancer Institute (NCI) recommends that women begin mammograms to screen for breast cancer starting at age forty. NCI claims that screening mammography reduces deaths from breast cancer even though it does not always prevent death. NCI claims that despite the risks of false-negative results, false-positive results, overdiagnosis, and radiation, mammograms and clinical exams are the most effective ways to detect breast cancer early. NCI is part of the National Institutes of Health in the US Department of Health and Human Services and the principal governmental agency for cancer research and training.

As you read, consider the following questions:

1. NCI claims that research indicates screening mammography can help reduce deaths from breast cancer for women in what age range?

National Cancer Institute, "Mammograms," July 24, 2012. www.cancer.gov.

2. According to NCI, false-negative mammography results do occur, missing what percent of breast cancers present?

3. NCI recommends that what population of women discuss with their health care providers the possibility of receiving mammograms before the age of forty?

A mammogram is an x-ray picture of the breast.

Using Mammograms for Screening and Diagnosis

Mammograms can be used to check for breast cancer in women who have no signs or symptoms of the disease. This type of mammogram is called a screening mammogram. Screening mammograms usually involve two x-ray pictures, or images, of each breast. The x-ray images make it possible to detect tumors that cannot be felt. Screening mammograms can also find microcalcifications (tiny deposits of calcium) that sometimes indicate the presence of breast cancer.

Mammograms can also be used to check for breast cancer after a lump or other sign or symptom of the disease has been found. This type of mammogram is called a diagnostic mammogram. Besides a lump, signs of breast cancer can include breast pain, thickening of the skin of the breast, nipple discharge, or a change in breast size or shape; however, these signs may also be signs of benign conditions. A diagnostic mammogram can also be used to evaluate changes found during a screening mammogram or to view breast tissue when it is difficult to obtain a screening mammogram because of special circumstances, such as the presence of breast implants.

Diagnostic mammography takes longer than screening mammography because more x-rays are needed to obtain views of the breast from several angles. The technician may magnify a suspicious area to produce a detailed picture that can help the doctor make an accurate diagnosis.

Benefits and Harms of Mammograms

Early detection of breast cancer with screening mammography means that treatment can be started earlier in the course of the disease, possibly before it has spread. Results from randomized clinical trials and other studies show that screening mammography can help reduce the number of deaths from breast cancer among women ages 40 to 70, especially for those over age 50. However, studies to date have not shown a benefit from regular screening mammography in women under age 40 or from baseline screening mammograms (mammograms used for comparison) taken before age 40.

Finding cancer early does not always reduce a woman's chance of dying from breast cancer. Even though mammograms can detect malignant tumors that cannot be felt, treating a small tumor does not always mean that the woman will not die from the cancer. A fast-growing or aggressive cancer may have already spread to other parts of the body before it is detected. Women with such tumors live a longer period of time knowing that they likely have a fatal disease.

In addition, screening mammograms may not help prolong the life of a woman who is suffering from other, more life-threatening health conditions.

The Cause of False-Negative Mammogram Results

False-negative results occur when mammograms appear normal even though breast cancer is present. Overall, screening mammograms miss about 20 percent of breast cancers that are present at the time of screening.

The main cause of false-negative results is high breast density. Breasts contain both dense tissue (i.e., glandular tissue

Breast Imaging Reporting and Database System (BI-RADS)

Category	Assessment	Follow-up
0	Need additional imaging evaluation	Additional imaging needed before a category can be assigned
1	Negative	Continue regular screening mammograms (for women over age 40)
2	Benign (noncancerous) finding	Continue regular screening mammograms (for women over age 40)
3	Probably benign	Receive a 6-month follow-up mammogram
4	Suspicious abnormality	May require biopsy
5	Highly suggestive of malignancy (cancer)	Requires biopsy
6	Known biopsy—proven malignancy (cancer)	Biopsy confirms presence of cancer before treatment begins

TAKEN FROM: National Cancer Institute, "Mammograms," July 24, 2012. www.cancer.gov.

and connective tissue, together known as fibroglandular tissue) and fatty tissue. Fatty tissue appears dark on a mammogram, whereas fibroglandular tissue appears as white areas. Because fibroglandular tissue and tumors have similar density, tumors can be harder to detect in women with denser breasts.

False-negative results occur more often among younger women than among older women because younger women are more likely to have dense breasts. As a woman ages, her breasts usually become more fatty, and false-negative results become less likely. False-negative results can lead to delays in treatment and a false sense of security for affected women.

The Cause of False-Positive Mammogram Results

False-positive results occur when radiologists decide mammograms are abnormal but no cancer is actually present. All abnormal mammograms should be followed up with additional testing (diagnostic mammograms, ultrasound, and/or biopsy) to determine whether cancer is present.

False-positive results are more common for younger women, women who have had previous breast biopsies, women with a family history of breast cancer, and women who are taking estrogen (for example, menopausal hormone therapy).

False-positive mammogram results can lead to anxiety and other forms of psychological distress in affected women. The additional testing required to rule out cancer can also be costly and time consuming and can cause physical discomfort.

The Harms of Overdiagnosis and Radiation

Screening mammograms can find cancers and cases of ductal carcinoma in situ (DCIS, a noninvasive tumor in which abnormal cells that may become cancerous build up in the lining of breast ducts) that need to be treated. However, they can also find cancers and cases of DCIS that will never cause symptoms or threaten a woman's life, leading to "overdiagnosis" of breast cancer. Treatment of these latter cancers and cases of DCIS is not needed and leads to "overtreatment." Overtreatment exposes women unnecessarily to the adverse effects associated with cancer therapy.

Because doctors often cannot distinguish cancers and cases of DCIS that need to be treated from those that do not, they are all treated.

Mammograms require very small doses of radiation. The risk of harm from this radiation exposure is extremely low, but repeated x-rays have the potential to cause cancer. The benefits of mammography, however, nearly always outweigh the potential harm from the radiation exposure. Nevertheless, women should talk with their health care providers about the need for each x-ray. In addition, they should always let their health care provider and the x-ray technician know if there is any possibility that they are pregnant, because radiation can harm a growing fetus.

Recommendations for Screening Mammograms

Women age 40 and older should have mammograms every 1 to 2 years.

Women who are at higher than average risk of breast cancer (for example, because of a family history of the disease or because they carry a known mutation in either the *BRCA1* or the *BRCA2* gene) should talk with their health care providers about whether to have mammograms before age 40 and how often to have them.

Getting a high-quality screening mammogram and having a clinical breast exam (an exam done by a health care provider) on a regular basis are the most effective ways to detect breast cancer early. As with any screening test, screening mammograms have both benefits and limitations. For example, some cancers cannot be detected by a screening mammogram but may be found by a clinical breast exam.

The Benefits of Self-Exams

Checking one's own breasts for lumps or other unusual changes is called a breast self-exam, or BSE. This type of exam cannot replace regular screening mammograms or clinical breast exams. In clinical trials, BSE alone was not found to help reduce the number of deaths from breast cancer.

Although regular BSE is not specifically recommended for breast cancer screening, many women choose to examine their own breasts. Women who do so should remember that breast changes can occur because of pregnancy, aging, menopause, during menstrual cycles, or when taking birth control pills or other hormones. It is normal for breasts to feel a little lumpy and uneven. Also, it is common for breasts to be swollen and tender right before or during a menstrual period. If a woman notices any unusual changes in her breasts, she should contact her health care provider.

The American College of Radiology (ACR) has established a uniform way for radiologists to describe mammogram findings. The system, called BI-RADS [Breast Imaging Reporting and Data System], includes seven standardized categories, or levels. Each BI-RADS category has a follow-up plan associated with it to help radiologists and other physicians appropriately manage a patient's care.

| "Tests aren't perfect. Some of them, in fact, are so far from perfect that you're safer not having them at all."

Why the PSA Test Is DOA

T.E. Holt

In the following viewpoint, T.E. Holt argues that the harms that can result from medical screening tests are often ignored. Holt claims that a recent recommendation from the US Preventive Services Task Force is based on sound evidence that the prostate-specific antigen (PSA) test may have more harms than benefits. Holt contends that biopsies and treatment for prostate cancer pose serious risks for a disease that, by itself, is not usually very serious, and he claims this is especially problematic because the PSA test has such a high rate of false results. Holt is an assistant professor in the Department of Social Medicine at the University of North Carolina at Chapel Hill School of Medicine.

As you read, consider the following questions:

1. According to the author, what are the two kinds of false results that a medical test can have?

2. Holt estimates that prostate-biopsy complications lead to approximately how many unnecessary hospitalizations each year due to false PSA results?

T.E. Holt, "Why the PSA Test Is DOA," *Men's Health*, vol. 27, no. 3, April 2012, p. 106.

3. What percent of men under sixty will die from radical prostatectomy, according to the author?

*H*e's a new patient, a man of about 40 who has borderline hypertension but is otherwise healthy. There are no skeletons in his family history; he is a nonsmoker, drinks occasionally, exercises frequently: a good bet to live to 101. As we're wrapping up, I suggest we order a screening lipid panel and a blood chemistry panel, but other than that there's nothing to do.

His face takes on a set expression I've come to recognize: He was expecting something else.

"What about a PSA test?" he says.

Despite my best efforts, I can feel one of my eyebrows start to rise. When I say, "Why?" I'm trying to sound neutral.

"My old doctor always did one," he explains, half apologetically. "Is there a problem?"

Last fall, the U.S. Preventive Services Task Force delivered its latest findings and recommendations on the prostate-specific antigen (PSA) test as a screening tool for prostate cancer. After reviewing the relevant research, it concluded that routine PSA screening does not prevent significantly more deaths than no screening—and that the results may lead to follow-up tests and treatments that could be unnecessary and even do harm. In other words, the research to date (and there has been a great deal of it) has failed to detect a meaningful benefit from routine screening for prostate cancer.

The task force's findings generated an intense public debate. The American Urological Association provided a letter for its members to send to local news media that asserted, "It would be barbaric to universally dismiss the PSA test before a suitable alternative to prostate cancer diagnosis is available. There are many men in this community who would tell you that a PSA test saved their life." Which was in fact true, as men and their doctors weighed in to support the PSA test in blog posts and op-ed pieces.

In an era when every medical guideline and practice is scrutinized by insurers, federal regulators, doctors, and patients looking to squeeze the most value from strained budgets, controversies such as this one will only become more common. At worst, as the sorry episode of the "death panel" publicity from a few years ago showed, these debates can degenerate into political opportunism and name-calling. At best, they offer a chance to understand how medicine works. And in the case of the PSA test, we're afforded a glimpse into a key aspect of medical care that few people understand, despite the often crucial role it plays in decisions that affect your health and safety.

He's been a patient of mine for a dozen years or so: a bit overweight, borderline diabetes, but not much given to worrying. This morning, though, he has a piece of paper in his hands, torn out of the morning daily.

"I think I need to go to this," he says, sliding the paper across the table.

I've seen the ad before. It's pitching a mobile diagnostic lab. The sales spiel promises to find the early warning signs of a variety of dangerous conditions, including coronary artery disease, stroke, hypertension, and diabetes—all four horsemen of your personal apocalypse.

Reading that list of mortal perils, I find myself growing anxious. The effect seems to have been even stronger on my patient.

"Do you think I should go?"

I glance up at the clock. My lunch break is just about gone. Ah, well.

What the PSA test and the mobile lab have in common is that they're being offered as what we call "screening tests." A screen is just what the name suggests: You take a pile of sand and sift it, and if you're lucky, something interesting hangs up in the mesh—gold, maybe, or some kind of intriguing fossil. What makes screening useful is that you don't have to look too hard at that pile of sand: Just scoop, dump, and shake. If

Benefits and Harms of Prostate-Specific Antigen (PSA) Cancer Screening

What are the benefits and harms of screening 1,000 men aged 55 to 69†
years old with a PSA test every 1 to 4 years for 10 years?

Possible benefit of screening	**Men, *n***
Reduced 10 year risk for dying of prostate cancer	
Die of prostate cancer with no screening	5 in 1,000
Die of prostate cancer with screening	4–5 in 1,000
Do not die of prostate cancer because of screening	0–1 in 1,000
Harms of screening	
At least 1 false-positive screening PSA test result	
Most positive test results lead to biopsy. Of men having biopsy, up to 33% will have moderate or major bothersome symptoms, including pain, fever, bleeding, infection, and temporary urinary difficulties; 1% will be hospitalized.	100–120 in 1,000
Prostate cancer diagnosis	
Although a diagnosis of prostate cancer may not be considered a harm, currently 90% of diagnosed men are treated and, thus, are at risk for the harms of treatment. A large majority of the men who are being treated would do well without treatment. A substantial percentage of these men would have remained asymptomatic for life.	110 in 1,000

(continued)

† The best evidence of possible benefit of PSA screening is in men aged 55–69 years.

TAKEN FROM: Virginia A. Moyer on behalf of the US Preventive Services Task Force, "Screening for Prostate Cancer: US Preventive Services Task Force Recommendation Statement," *Annals of Internal Medicine*, vol. 157, no. 2, July 17, 2012, p. 124.

Benefits and Harms of Prostate-Specific Antigen (PSA) Cancer Screening (continued)

Harms of screening (cont.)

Complications of treatment (among persons who are screened)‡

Develop serious cardiovascular events due to treatment	2 in 1,000
Develop deep venous thrombosis or pulmonary embolus due to treatment	1 in 1,000
Develop erectile dysfunction due to treatment	29 in 1,000
Develop urinary incontinence due to treatment	18 in 1,000
Die due to treatment	<1 in 1,000

‡ The rate of complications depends on the proportion of men having treatment and the method of treatment. The table reflects a distribution of 60% surgical treatment, 30% radiation, and 10% observation. Other harms of radiation, such as bowel damage, are not shown.

TAKEN FROM: Virginia A. Moyer on behalf of the US Preventive Services Task Force, "Screening for Prostate Cancer: US Preventive Services Task Force Recommendation Statement," *Annals of Internal Medicine*, vol. 157, no. 2, July 17, 2012, p. 124.

---

you want to go through a lot of sand in a hurry, it's a great method. The only problem, as anyone who has tried this knows, is that 999 times out of a thousand all that's left on the screen is an old stick and a cigarette butt.

Some medical tests function as screens by design, and the principle is pretty much the same. You know that somewhere out in the population are a few people who have a certain disease. You don't know who they are, and you don't have time to examine every individual in detail, so you screen. You try to test everybody at risk—in the case of prostate cancer, all men 50 and older (and some in their 40s if they have specific risk factors). The point of screening is to find that cancer before its symptoms appear—ideally, the thinking goes, when it's still early enough to treat.

So why, then, would the government switch course on the PSA? And why do I recommend that my patients stay out of mobile labs?

This has to do with an inescapable fact about medical tests, a truth so simple we have a hard time keeping it in focus: Tests aren't perfect. Some of them, in fact, are so far from perfect that you're safer not having them at all.

Simply undergoing a test—any test—poses a risk. There are obvious things to worry about: An invasive test can nick an artery, introduce infection, [or] puncture something vital. But even tests that don't involve more than an ordinary blood draw carry risk. The risk here is of a different kind, subtler, but very real all the same. The risk I'm talking about arises when the test tells you something that isn't true.

People sometimes fear (usually but not always needlessly) that a test might say you're healthy when you're actually sick. Technically, this kind of mistake is called a false negative: It's the kind of thing that can keep people up nights worrying that the doctor missed something. Most of us have an immediate grasp of how this presents a problem, and in fact the PSA test does have a high false-negative rate. One of the points the task force made against retaining the PSA test as a routine screening measure wasn't how often it fails to find cancer, however. It was something most of us find a little harder to see as a risk: how often the results say you're sick when actually you're not. This is called a false positive.

Screening tests have built-in rates of false negatives and false positives. Usually the two are inversely related, like the ends of a seesaw: A test with a low rate of false negatives generally returns a lot of false positives, and vice versa. Using a test with a high rate of false negatives would have little point: So many people would slip through the net that you'd be just as efficient letting cases be diagnosed based on symptoms. For that reason, most screening tests have a low rate of false negatives, and therefore a high rate of false positives.

But the most remarkable consequence of the PSA test is the sheer quantity of false positives. An estimated 240,890 new cases of prostate cancer were diagnosed last year. Assuming that the PSA had false-positive and false-negative rates of 10 percent each (and in reality neither rate is that good), and that you managed to screen the entire at-risk population in the United States, that translates into *4.5 million false-positive results.*

It's bad enough that 4.5 million men would receive a call telling them they might have prostate cancer. But what happens next is worse. Usually following a positive screening test is a second, far more accurate test, one that's typically more complicated and expensive. In this two-step process, the initial screen picks out possible cases of disease, and a second confirmatory test figures out which of those possible cases are real. It's the nature of the confirmatory test that follows a positive PSA test that makes the false-positive rate a serious problem.

That test is called a transrectal biopsy, and it's just as nasty as it sounds: Twelve samples of tissue are punched out of a man's prostate through his rectum. Estimates of harm arising directly from this test are difficult to pin down, but the known side effects include serious infections that are sometimes bad enough to lead to death: The hospitalization rate for prostate-biopsy complications is about 2 percent. Those 4.5 million false positives could be responsible for 90,000 hospitalizations a year.

The task force viewed all this pain and loss as too high a price to pay for the cancers the PSA test has caught. Which perspective you take depends on whom you ask, but these recommendations weigh the number of men harmed by false diagnoses against the much smaller number of men correctly diagnosed—and contend that there's no benefit.

This is due not only to the rate of biopsy complications but also (and more importantly) to the fact that while the PSA test may catch cancers, it probably does nothing to save lives. The difference in death rates between men regularly screened for prostate cancer with the test and men who aren't turns out to be so small that it's indistinguishable from a statistical error. And since the risk of dying of prostate cancer is very low to begin with, the task force argued that the benefit of testing (if one exists) doesn't justify putting men who happen to have a positive PSA test result through the risks and rigors of a prostate biopsy.

The extreme variability of prostate cancers adds yet another element of uncertainty. Some grow rapidly, but many evolve so slowly that you can live with cancer in your prostate for years and never know it: You'll grow old and die of something else. This slow-growing form is so common, in fact, that the debate is now shifting to whether we should treat it like a disease at all. And even the difference in prostate cancers may not be that significant: While results from a large European screening trial indicate that unscreened men tended to develop more aggressive cancers than PSA-tested men do, the most recent results of a similarly large U.S. trial found no difference in overall death rates between the two groups.

So given the current state of science, we have no reliable answer to the ultimate question: Do we test for this or let it alone? Judging by the similar results you'd receive by taking either of the two paths, it's hard to believe the biopsy adds anything to guide that decision. Throw this aspect of prostate cancer into the mix, and the value of the test becomes very hard to find.

More men live with prostate cancer than die of it. But what kind of life you live along the way depends radically on how aggressively you treat the cancer. The task force concluded that the treatments for prostate cancer have left far too many men suffering not from the disease but from its treatment.

The range of dangers lurking behind a positive PSA test result include events most of us would be unlikely to choose as preferable to the disease itself. The effects of prostatectomy and other treatments such as radiation include incontinence, erectile dysfunction, genitals too numb for sensation (pleasurable or not), and chronic inflammation of the rectum.

If those aren't enough to make you think twice, consider this: The American College of Cardiology calculates the risk of heart attack during any urologic surgery at 4 percent. And the mortality rates from radical prostatectomy hover around 0.2 percent for men under 60. Heart attack, incontinence, a 1-in-500 chance of dying from a procedure that may do nothing to prolong your life: The list is enough to make a man think he's made a bad bargain.

Bear in mind that regular PSA testing is still warranted for certain men—those who have had prostate cancer and therefore need to take necessary precautions against the return of their disease. The likelihood of recurrent cancer in those men is much higher than the chance of finding cancer in the population at large, and under those circumstances the problem of false positives plays out differently. For men in this group, a positive PSA test is cause for genuine concern, though by no means a sign that the end is near.

He's another new patient, a hard-bodied, squash-playing nonsmoker, VP for finance in a major computing firm. He's in his late 40s, with nothing much in his history except frequent insomnia. He fidgets on the exam table, glancing at his watch more often than I check mine. On his intake form he indicated that he drinks six to eight cups of coffee a day, and two to three glasses of wine every night with dinner.

We talk a little about the insomnia, which I suggest might improve with less caffeine and alcohol. He shakes his head impatiently and asks instead for a prescription for a heavily marketed sedative-hypnotic. I explain my reluctance to do this until after he's tried to cut down on the things that are actually keeping him awake.

The look he gives me is clearly one of annoyance. I take a minute while I tick off the boxes on the lab form to think about how I can improve what's starting out as a rocky relationship.

"Is that all?" he asks. Despite myself, I can feel that eyebrow twitching upward.

"My old doctor usually ordered an EKG."

"I noticed that." Among his medical records are about a dozen electrocardiograms, every one normal. I silently review everything he's told me about his family history.

I hold up the sheaf of cardiograms. "Did your doctor ever explain why you needed all these?"

"No," he replies with another look at his watch. "It was just part of the standard exam."

For a moment I'm tempted. The easier thing to do, after all, would be just to order the test. What harm could it do?

Oh, lots. A faulty placement of the leads, an uninterpretably shaky baseline, any number of random electrical or physiologic artifacts could produce an abnormal EKG. At which point you have to decide either to ignore the test, or go on to the next step, which is where the slippery slope begins. No, I tell him. Given everything I know about you, any abnormal result would more likely be instrument error than anything else.

I'm not sure how much luck I had explaining this. Or if he's going to come back. He may not need an EKG, but he does need a doctor.

Medical testing is synonymous, in a lot of ways, with what most of us mean when we talk about medical technology. The phrase conjures up a vague, shiny image of expensive machinery, holographic displays of body parts floating in space, and white-coated savants huddled around, nodding sagely. Even something as humble as a blood test like that used to measure PSA levels requires an autoimmune analyzer, a device that might have come from the prop department of the old *Star Trek* series.

Medical testing also tends to conjure a sense of medicine out of control, of costs rising faster than we can afford to pay. And finally, it raises questions: Are we reaping meaningful benefits from all that technology? Does the cardiac PET scanner really tell us more than we used to glean from an echocardiogram, an EKG, or even a trained ear with a stethoscope? If the autoimmune analyzer tells me the answer is 7, how do I know if I'm even asking the right question?

All the technology and numbers in the world are no substitute for clinical judgment. One way to know when you have a good doctor is when you find one who's able to tell you not just the numbers but what they mean and what they don't mean—and who is sometimes willing to say, "That test isn't right for you," and to tell you why. This conversation takes a certain amount of faith, and trust, on both your parts. Neither is something to be taken for granted. But both are, in the right hands, the best medicine there can be.

The identifying characteristics of patients described in this essay have been altered to protect patient privacy. Any resemblance between such descriptions and any specific individual, living or dead, is a coincidence.

The Medical Test Every Man Needs

You don't have to roll up your sleeve, but you do have to pull down your. . .

Doctors may debate the merits of other medical tests, but there's little disagreement on the colonoscopy. It's highly reliable. Best of all, the scope can remove abnormal intestinal growths, literally nipping any precancerous process in the bud (and providing a definitive diagnosis as well). True, the aftermath of drinking a gallon of fluids and taking a powerful laxative isn't fun. But that inconvenience, and the relatively low risk of complications, is worth the price of admission to your posterior. Consider: One in 19 men reading this will develop colon cancer; one in 47 will die of it. This is why gastroenterologists I know say, "No one in this country should ever die of colon cancer." If you're over 50 (or have close relatives with colon polyps or cancer), you need this test.

> "The findings ... suggest nearly half of all deaths from prostate cancer can be predicted before age 50."

Researchers: PSA Test Saves Lives, Government Guidelines Are Wrong

Nick Tate

In the following viewpoint, Nick Tate argues that a recent recommendation from the US Preventive Services Task Force discouraging use of the prostate-specific antigen (PSA) test will do more harm to men than good. Tate claims that since the advent of the PSA test, the rates of metastatic prostate cancer and prostate cancer mortality have dropped, speaking in favor of its use. Tate claims that the decision to use the PSA test should be made on an individual basis and should not be discouraged. Nick Tate is an editor at Newsmax.

As you read, consider the following questions:

1. What is the United States Preventive Services Task Force and what did they reccommend, according to the author?

2. As stated by the author, what is the Malmo study? What was the purpose of this study?

3. According to Tate, what does Dr. Samedi say is the recommended age to start PSA testing?

Men with high PSA test results as early as age 45 are three times more likely to develop a life-threatening form of prostate cancer than those with lower levels, according to a new study that provides fresh evidence that the controversial screening method can benefit younger men.

Despite new federal guidelines issued last year that recommend against routine PSA testing for men at any age, an international team of U.S. and Swedish researchers found the risk of being diagnosed with an aggressive prostate cancer that spreads to other parts of the body and bone within 15 years is three-fold higher for men aged 45–49 with elevated PSA levels than those with lower concentrations.

What's more, the risk of developing metastatic prostate cancer is 10 times greater for men aged 51–55 with high PSA test results. Taken together, the findings—published in the *British Medical Journal*—suggest nearly half of all deaths from prostate cancer can be predicted before age 50. What's more, initiating PSA screening after then may leave many men at risk of being diagnosed with an incurable form of cancer, the researchers found.

"Measurement of PSA concentration in early midlife can identify a small group of men at increased risk of prostate cancer metastasis several decades later," the researchers concluded. "Careful surveillance is warranted in these men."

David Samadi, M.D., vice chairman of the Department of Urology and Chief of Robotics and Minimally Invasive Surgery at the Mount Sinai School of Medicine in New York City, tells Newsmax Health the findings provide a strong endorsement of PSA testing. That's particularly true for men in their

40s who have an increased cancer risk because of their family history, genetics, race, and other factors.

"We know the PSA test has reduced the mortality of cancer by 40 percent, so it has been an effective test," said Dr. Samadi. "Of course we need a better test. But 10, 15 years ago we used to see people coming in with metastatic [cancer], where it had spread to other parts of the body and spread to the bone, but we don't see that that much anymore."

PSA (prostate-specific antigen) is a protein produced by cells of the prostate gland. PSA is often elevated in men with cancer, and the test was originally approved by the U.S. Food and Drug Administration in 1986 to track the progression of cancer in men diagnosed with it. In 1994, the FDA approved the use of the PSA test with a digital rectal exam (DRE) to test asymptomatic men for prostate cancer.

But an elevated PSA does not necessarily indicate the presence of prostate cancer. It can also flag other non-cancerous conditions, such as prostatitis (inflammation of the prostate) and benign prostatic hyperplasia (enlargement of the prostate).

Most doctors consider PSA levels of 4.0 nanograms of PSA per mililiter (ng/mL) of blood and lower to be normal. Those with PSAs of 4.0 or higher are often sent for a prostate biopsy to check for cancer.

Until recently, many doctors and health organizations encouraged yearly PSA screening for most men beginning at age 50. But recent studies have shown that some men with PSA levels below 4.0 have prostate cancer, while many men with higher levels do not have prostate cancer.

Last year, the United States Preventive Services Task Force—an independent panel of experts authorized by Congress—issued new recommendations against routine PSA screening, regardless of age, for men without cancer symptoms.

But the new study raises questions about those guidelines. For the study, researchers examined medical data from the

The Decision to Undergo PSA Testing

Decisions regarding early detection of prostate cancer should be individualized, and benefits and consequences should be discussed with the patient before PSA testing occurs. Not all men are appropriate candidates for screening efforts for this disease. Ideally, physicians should consider a number of factors, including patient age and comorbidity, as well as preferences for the relevant potential outcomes. Screening in men with less than a 10-year life expectancy, either due to age or comorbidity, is discouraged. Some organizations have even recommended that informed consent should be obtained prior to PSA testing.

"Prostate-Specific Antigen Best Practice Statement:
2009 Update," American Urological Association, 2009.

long-running Malmo Preventative Project to determine who might benefit most from PSA testing—and at what age. A previous study using MPP data, published in the BMJ in 2010, demonstrated that PSA level at age 60 can predict the risk of death from prostate cancer by age 85.

The Malmo study included 21,277 men, aged 27 to 52, who participated in the MPP between 1974 and 1984. All gave blood samples to be tested for PSA levels. The results showed 44 percent of deaths among the men from prostate cancer occurred in those with the top 10 percent of PSA levels at age 45–49—a PSA of 1.5 ng/ml or more.

In fact, the risk of developing metastatic prostate cancer within 15 years was three times higher for men in the top level PSA at age 45–49 and 10 times higher at age 51–55. This suggests that initiating PSA screening after age 50 would leave many men at risk of later being diagnosed with an incurable cancer. But even men with the highest PSA levels at age 40 had a very low risk of developing metastatic prostate cancer within 15 years, indicating PSA testing is not justified at that age for most men.

Dr. Samadi noted the study finds PSA testing is beneficial, but must be conducted and analyzed by a doctor who specializes in its use and that it be done over a period of time to track patterns and trends.

"There's an art to managing the PSA test and it should be handled by doctors who use the PSA all the time," he said. "I don't just look at the value alone, but I look at the trend over time."

He recommends men start the PSA screening at 45, as a baseline, then get a PSA once a year afterward. Some men at increased risk for cancer should start PSA screening at 40—including African-Americans, those with a family history of the disease, and men with variations in the genes BRCA1 and BRCA2 (tied to both prostate and breast cancer).

"Medicine is really like detective work," Dr. Samadi explains. "You have to use the art to decide who should have the PSA test and who should not. You have to look at the [results of] a physical exam, the race, family history, then the genetic package . . . and then decide who should be screened."

"The specialty boards seem to now recognize that the results of testing include both signals (useful information) and noise (false and distracting information)."

Medical Boards Are Recommending That Doctors Cut Back on Medical Tests

H. Gilbert Welch

In the following viewpoint, H. Gilbert Welch argues that the 2012 recommendations from medical specialty boards and societies advising against certain medical tests is a good start toward ending unnecessary medical diagnosis and treatment. Welch claims that although the recommendations are promising, more needs to be done to fix the medical system that pushes doctors to perform unnecessary tests. Welch is a professor of medicine at the Dartmouth Institute for Health Policy and Clinical Practice and author of Overdiagnosed: Making People Sick in the Pursuit of Health.

As you read, consider the following questions:

1. According to Welch, how many specialty societies contributed recommendations to a 2012 list that advocated cutting back on certain tests and treatments?

2. Which two recommendations against medical tests have been around for years, yet are frequently ignored, according to the author?

3. Welch claims that the legal system pushes doctors to overuse tests for what reason?

In case you missed it, a recommendation came out last month [April 2012] that physicians cut back on using 45 common tests and treatments. In addition, patients were advised to question doctors who recommend such things as antibiotics for mild sinusitis, CT [computed tomography] scans for an uncomplicated headache or a repeat colonoscopy within 10 years of a normal exam.

Medical Professionals Recommend Fewer Tests

The general idea wasn't all that new—my colleagues and I have been questioning many of the same tests and treatments for years. What was different this time was the source of the recommendations. They came from the heart of the medical profession: the medical specialty boards and societies representing cardiologists, radiologists, gastroenterologists and other doctors. In other words, they came from the very groups that stand to benefit from doing more, not less.

Nine specialty societies contributed five recommendations each to the list (others are expected to contribute in the future). The recommendations each started with the word "don't"—as in "don't perform," "don't order," "don't recommend."

Could American medicine be changing?

For years, medical organizations have been developing recommendations and guidelines focused on things doctors should do. The specialty societies have been focused on protecting the financial interests of their most profligate members and have been reluctant to acknowledge the problem of overuse. Maybe they are now owning up to the problem.

And judging from the content of the list, testing is a big part of that problem. Only a quarter of the recommendations fell in the category of "don't treat"—as in, don't prescribe more chemotherapy for end-stage cancer that is beyond hope. The remainder fell in the category of "don't test."

The Problem with Routine Medical Testing

Because it can be the first step in a cascade of medical interventions, the focus on testing makes good sense. The specialty boards seem to now recognize that the results of testing include both signals (useful information) and noise (false and distracting information). For patients with symptoms the signal predominates. But for those without symptoms the noise predominates. And the noise is not harmless; it can trigger overdiagnosis and overtreatment. "Routine" chest X-rays, for example, have a way of unearthing multiple abnormalities. This raises questions in physicians' minds—triggering CT scans, needle biopsies, bronchoscopies and even surgery in an effort to answer them.

That's why multiple recommendations have argued against routine use of tests such as cardiograms (EKGs), ECHO [echocardiograms] and CT scans in asymptomatic patients—and against repetitive testing in patients whose symptoms have not changed.

Admittedly, some of the recommendations seem brain-dead obvious.

Don't screen for cancer in dying patients. (How could they possibly benefit from the early detection of a cancer that will not have time to progress?)

Don't screen for cervical cancer in women who don't have a cervix. (How could they possibly be at risk for cancer in an organ they no longer have?)

You might think such guidance would be unneeded. Sadly, research using the Medicare data has demonstrated both those things regularly occur.

Other recommendations have been around for years. Don't order CT scans and MRIs [magnetic resonance imaging scans] on patients with nonspecific low back pain. Don't order routine preoperative chest X-rays. Yet those orders continue.

Good Doctors Are Working in a Bad System

Most doctors will agree with the recommendations on the list. But the problem of overuse is less one of bad doctors (although there are a few); the problem is more one of good doctors working in a bad system.

The truth is there are many forces that push us to do more. There are the performance measures that typically give doctors good grades for ordering tests, rather than for not ordering them. There is the legal system that will punish us for underdiagnosis, but not for overdiagnosis. There are the demands from patients seeking to get their money's worth from insurance after years of being taught to believe the best medical care is the most medical care. And there are the financial rewards: Most doctors, and/or the clinics and hospitals they work for, are paid more if they do more.

But we have to start somewhere—and this list is a good start. Now it needs to be extended.

Personally, I would have liked to see the recommendation "Don't perform breast or prostate cancer screening unless the patient understands both the harms and benefits." Or perhaps we could think even more broadly: "Don't feel compelled to end every patient encounter with an order for a test, a recommendation for a procedure or a prescription for a medication."

| "*Health care should never be the currency that the powerful get to trade in.*"

Recommendations to Cut Back on Medical Tests Are Unfair

Hal Scherz

In the following viewpoint, Hal Scherz argues that recent government recommendations regarding medical testing will lead to an unjust distribution of health care. Scherz warns that with the growth in government control of health care due to the Affordable Care Act, only wealthy Americans will receive thorough health care. Scherz is the founder and president of Docs4Patient Care, an organization of concerned physicians committed to the establishment of a health-care system that preserves the sanctity of the doctor-patient relationship, promotes quality of care, supports affordable access to all Americans, and protects patients' freedom of choice.

As you read, consider the following questions:

1. According to the author, in 2011 what agency recommended against routine screening for prostate cancer in healthy men?

2. Scherz anticipates that government restrictions on cancer screening will soon be extended to what procedure?

3. According to Scherz, what percent of physicians want to see the Affordable Care Act, also known as ObamaCare, repealed?

One of life's minor annoyances occurs when someone receives preferential treatment because of his wealth or perceived power. Many people have experienced this firsthand when a "VIP" comes into a restaurant and jumps ahead while they've been waiting for a table. This offends most Americans because it is contrary to our sense of fair play. It divides people into elites and everyone else.

The Impact of Government on Health Care

This is where we are heading with health care. Don't think so? Well, on October 11, 2011, the U.S. Preventative Services Task Force (USPSTF) declared that PSA [prostate specific antigen] screening for prostate cancer in healthy men was no longer recommended. No urologists—the acknowledged experts in the treatment of prostate cancer—were involved in this decision. During the time that PSA screening has been available, prostate cancer deaths have steadily declined. Then why have these recommendations been issued? Because in a top-down, government-controlled health care system, dollars need to be trimmed and patients cannot get everything that they want, even when it means screening for cancer. Patients have no say over their health care, and the government decides where health care dollars are allocated—perhaps instead to Planned Parenthood for abortions. Incidentally, President [Barack] Obama underwent PSA screening several months ago.

During the contentious debates over the Affordable Care Act, the SEIU [Service Employees International Union] and other unions which were staunch Obama allies spent tens of millions of dollars to produce marketing campaigns in sup-

The Danger of Government Guidelines

Who should get a mammogram? At what age? How frequently? What about Pap smears and prostate cancer tests and colonoscopies? Aren't these questions experts can decide? Unfortunately, no. Any reader of daily newspapers knows that we are forever getting conflicting advice from well-meaning people. Part of the problem is that people differ in their attitude toward risk. They also differ in their willingness to spend money to reduce risk. A danger in a one-size-fits-all approach fashioned in Washington, D.C., is that the experts may not share your values. Their attitude toward risk reduction may be different from yours.

National Center for Policy Analysis,
"What Does Health Reform Mean for You?
A Consumer's Guide," updated September 2012.
www.ncpa.org.

port of passage of the bill. As [House Minority Leader] Nancy Pelosi has so ineloquently stated, "we need to pass the bill to find out what is in it." And once we did and learned how much it was going to cost, these devoted supporters discovered that they couldn't afford ObamaCare and flooded the Department of Health and Human Services with a tsunami of requests to exempt them from the new law. To date, 1,231 waivers have been granted as political favors, many to the very groups who were instrumental in getting the law passed. This includes 38 waivers granted in a single day in Nancy Pelosi's district—many to fancy nightclubs, swank hotels, and expensive restaurants which advertise $59 Porterhouse steaks.

If ObamaCare stands, and once fully implemented in 2014, ordinary men will no longer receive PSA screening; women will no longer receive routine mammography looking for breast cancer (a 2010 USPSTF recommendation); and soon these government restrictions on cancer screening will likely extend to colonoscopy, as occurs in several Canadian provinces, where routine screening is no longer offered. Seniors will wait longer for life-saving procedures like dialysis, heart surgery, or chemotherapy. Surgeries that improve quality of life like joint replacement will be denied outright. How can this not be the case when ObamaCare raids Medicare and steals $500 billion from it to be redistributed elsewhere?

ObamaCare Will Lead to Class Warfare

Currently, the federal government pays for over 50% of the health care delivered in America. If Progressives like Obama get their way, we will move to a single-payer, government-run health care system. This of course matters little to people like Barack Obama and Nancy Pelosi, who have the power to circumvent the intrusive laws that they are responsible for getting passed. For those who cannot get needed health care from the government but can afford to go elsewhere for it, they will do what Newfoundland premier Danny Williams did in 2010, when he came to Miami for heart surgery because it was unavailable to him in the government-run Canadian medical system.

It is not surprising that during President Obama's State of the Union address [2012], there was no mention of the Affordable Care Act—the singular "accomplishment" of his presidency. Obama wants to avoid bringing health care back into the public arena during this election season, knowing that only 25% of Americans believe that their health care will be better under ObamaCare, according to a recent Kaiser Foundation survey. This is a number similar to the 77% of physicians who want to see ObamaCare repealed. Instead, Obama will rely on the strategy of economic class warfare, pitting the 99-percenters against the so-called rich. What the president and his minions shamelessly engage in is another type of class warfare—those who must comply with the laws and those who are above them. Health care should never be the currency that the powerful get to trade in.

Periodical and Internet Sources Bibliography

The following articles have been selected to supplement the diverse views presented in this chapter.

| Christie Aschwanden | "The Risk-Benefit Calculation of Mammograms," *Slate*, December 10, 2012. www.slate.com. |

| Archie Bleyer and H. Gilbert Welch | "Effect of Three Decades of Screening Mammography on Breast-Cancer Incidence," *New England Journal of Medicine*, November 22, 2012. |

| David Catron | "A Gut Check on What Obama Means by 'Fairness,'" *American Spectator*, August 8, 2012. www.spectator.org. |

| Denise Cummins | "Mammograms and PSA Tests: What Your Doctor Needs to Tell You," *Psychology Today*, May 24, 2012. www.psychologytoday.com. |

| Madeline Haller | "The PSA Test: Do You Need It?," *Men's Health*, May 24, 2012. www.menshealth.com. |

| Paul Hsieh | "Is President Obama's Prostate Gland More Important than Yours?," *Forbes*, July 5, 2012. www.forbes.com. |

| Meri Kolbrener | "Are Mammograms Useless? A New Study Claims Mammograms Overdiagnose Breast Cancer," *Slate*, December 5, 2012. www.slate.com. |

| Tony Lobl | "Cancer Testing—Yes or No? Either Way, Screen Out the Fear," *Independent* (UK), December 4, 2012. |

| H. Gilbert Welch | "Testing What We Think We Know," *New York Times*, August 19, 2012. |

OPPOSING
VIEWPOINTS®
SERIES

CHAPTER 4

What Are Some Concerns About Genetic Testing?

Chapter Preface

Scientific knowledge about human genetics has been rapidly advancing over the last few decades. Genetic research has led to the development of genetic tests that can provide information about disease by analyzing DNA (deoxyribonucleic acid), RNA (ribonucleic acid), or protein. Genetic testing can confirm or rule out a suspected genetic condition, and it can help determine a person's chance of developing or passing on a genetic disorder. Approximately one thousand genetic tests are currently in use, and more are being developed. For now, the primary uses of genetic tests are for specific diseases where gene alteration has been positively linked with disease.

The purposes of genetic testing are controversial. Testing can be used to confirm diagnosis of a disease or to predict disease. Although the purpose of confirming a diagnosis of a disease is relatively free of controversy, other purposes based on prediction are rife with debate.

Using genetic testing to predict disease is not an exact science. Predictive and presymptomatic genetic tests are used to find gene changes that increase the likelihood of developing a particular disease, but the test cannot predict conclusively whether a person will get the disease. For this reason, the testing is controversial because the practical import of the test results is unclear. With the current inability to change one's genes in any way, finding out that one has a high likelihood of a disease may be psychologically challenging without resulting in any clear plan of action. For prenatal screening, there is the option of abortion, but this additional practical application makes the testing even more controversial for those who oppose abortion.

Given the limited benefits that predictive genetic testing confers at the present time, there are competing views about the wisdom of such testing. Concerns range from that of costliness without practical import to more extreme concerns about the dangers of such information. Nonetheless, there are many proponents of predictive genetic testing because it can allow parents who both carry genes for a particular disorder to seek ways to avoid having children with a high propensity for a particular disease. Additionally, such testing may not be solely predictive for long, with the advancement of genetic technologies promising gene therapy treatments that may treat or cure disease.

"*This bioethical issue is not merely philosophical, but deeply personal for millions of us, both as individuals and as responsible members of our families.*"

Genetic Testing for Incurable Diseases Poses Risks to Consumers and Families

Gregory Pence

In the following viewpoint, Greg Pence argues that there are ethical problems with testing people for the presence of genes that could lead to incurable diseases. Pence contends that genetic tests for Alzheimer's disease pose several problems, one of which is that testing is always a family affair, because genetic propensity to disease runs in families. Pence concludes that ethical concerns should lead to caution in going forward with presymptomatic genetic testing. Pence is a professor and chair of the Department of Philosophy at the University of Alabama at Birmingham.

As you read, consider the following questions:

1. According to the author, does the presence of the gene-variant called APOE4 mean that an individual will get Alzheimer's disease?

2. Pence cautions that inaccurate information from pre-symptomatic genetic testing from Alzheimer's could lead to what further ethical problems?

3. According to Pence, how many Alzheimer's patients are there predicted to be in 2050?

Few jobs exist where you might function while losing your mind. Few families exist where a mother's losing her mind wouldn't be devastating.

Genetic Testing Can Cause Emotional Harm

For decades, bioethicists have pondered whether patients should be told about a future disease. Each year, more accurate pre-symptomatic tests arrive, but do we want to know their results?

Previously, we knew that patients with one copy of a gene-variant called APOE4 develop Alzheimer's three times more than normal, and if they have two copies, twelve times more. Although 40 percent of Alzheimer's patients have this gene-variant, having it does not mean one gets Alzheimer's.

Recently, a California neurologist used MRI [magnetic resonance imaging] scans, combined with information from spinal taps, to better predict Alzheimer's. Right now, these tests still lack certainty, but soon we'll get there. But do we want to know?

Huntington's disease is like Alzheimer's in that it has no cure, but unlike Alzheimer's, it has a single gene that we can test for. Nevertheless, its ethical issues may presage those of testing for Alzheimer's.

First, getting the news is irreversible. You can't take it back. Once you know you have Huntington's, you cannot return to blissful ignorance.

Second, many people take the test to learn they lack the disease. That means that about half find out the opposite and are not emotionally prepared. Although people say they test to find out "my condition, either way," no one wants to hear bad news. Before clients take the test, genetic counselors try to make them feel if they can handle bad news, but most people don't get such counseling.

Testing Is a Family Affair

Third, testing is a family affair, and this is tricky. Medical and legal ethics emphasize a patient's autonomy, i.e. [that is], her right to know and to make decisions about her life and body. But, for better or worse, we are not atomistic individuals. We are spouses, parents, children and siblings. If we develop Alzheimer's, others must care for us. Don't they have the right to know, too?

Testing is a family affair in another way. Because Alzheimer's looks to be in part gene-based, testing one family member tells others about his or her risk.

Perhaps a lesson can be drawn from psychologist Nancy Wexler, whose mother died of Huntington's and who led the team that discovered tests for Huntington's. Convinced for decades that she would take the test when she could, instead, she later declined to take the test that she helped develop. She then advocated not taking it.

"If you have the gene," Wexler said, "it's not whether you will find out, but when."

So Wexler argued that, until the disease strikes, people should live robustly in ignorance. Otherwise, they may develop a sick identity. The news that they will develop Alzheimer's may overshadow everything, making them change long-term plans and do foolish things.

Testing for Incurable Diseases

A fourth lesson from the history of bioethics is that, in our capitalistic society, companies will try to make money selling presymptomatic tests for Alzheimer's—the way they do now for breast cancer and other multi-factorial diseases.

Understanding Alzheimer's Disease

Alzheimer's disease is an illness of the brain. It causes large numbers of nerve cells in the brain to die. This affects a person's ability to remember things, think clearly, and use good judgment.

Doctors don't know what causes the disease. They do know that most of the time it begins after age 60. Nearly half of people age 85 and older may have Alzheimer's.

Alzheimer's disease often starts slowly. In fact, some people don't know they have it. They blame their forgetfulness on old age. However, over time, their memory problems get more serious.

National Institute on Aging, "Understanding Alzheimer's Disease: What You Need to Know," August 2011. www.nia.nih.gov.

Such testing may convey inaccurate information and lead to further ethical problems, such as unnecessary suicides or people testing positive and then purchasing long-term coverage without disclosing it, bankrupting insurance companies. This is especially true when tests merely reveal increased risk of getting Alzheimer's, not certainty.

A final lesson from the history of bioethics is the consensus that if you can't offer a patient anything to prevent or to ameliorate a terrible disease, why test for it? For newborns with diseases such as Phenylketonuria (PKU), we can test, intervene and prevent bad effects, but as of now, this is not true for Alzheimer's or Huntington's.

Promoting Long-Term Health Coverage

There are many myths about Alzheimer's. It is likely to be caused both by genes and environmental factors, and to have variable courses. As someone who, with his wife, for a decade cared for a relative with dementia, I know that the benign portrait of dementia depicted in many movies and TV shows is inaccurate.

The federal government recently announced a commission to plan for the overwhelming number of future Alzheimer's patients. Unfortunately, this commission merely hopes to prevent or delay Alzheimer's, rather than plan for the care of those afflicted.

As a matter of intergenerational justice, can we expect our kids to pay for (the predicted) 13 million Alzheimer's patients in 2050, each of whom after diagnosis will probably live eight years? What about the elderly singleton without a living family? Clearly, we need a plan.

One little-noticed part of President Barack Obama's new national medical plan is the ability to purchase long-term health coverage from the government (patients must pay five years before they can use it). Given how few Americans have such coverage, and given how Medicare does not provide it, most of us should buy it.

Genetics Testing Impacts Individuals and Families

Discussing Alzheimer's with a relative of mine, he replied, "I'm in the Hemlock Society. Just kill me when I get it." Would that it were so simple. In all states, killing-with-consent is a crime, even if the loved one has a terminal illness.

Another friend says, "If I'm getting Alzheimer's, I'll kill myself." Maybe. But people in the early stages mask and deny their disease. It can take years for the disease to cripple a mind, and by that time, the person who would have killed himself is, quite simply, gone, replaced by a different being with half his former IQ who now wants to live.

It may seem I'm completely against testing by individuals, because knowledge has few benefits for them. But families also matter. It will be hard for them to stand by passively, watching a relative dissolve a good marriage, squandering retirement funds or making a bad will. Practically speaking, because the family must take responsibility for care, at some point, it must intervene to protect assets, both social and financial. But here it's a matter not of advance, presymptomatic testing, but of diagnosis of a disease. That's the right time to force testing, especially because drugs such as donepezil may then delay progression of the disease for six months.

So this bioethical issue is not merely philosophical, but deeply personal for millions of us, both as individuals and as responsible members of our families.

> *"The only people who seem especially overwrought and unable to handle the results of genetic testing are bioethicists."*

Consumers Do Not Need to Be Protected from Genetic Information

Ronald Bailey

In the following viewpoint, Ronald Bailey argues that it is misguided for bioethicists to try to protect people from genetic testing. Bailey claims that bioethicists' worries that people will suffer bad psychological effects from the knowledge gained from genetic testing are not borne out by scientific studies examining the effects. Bailey contends that individuals should have the right to decide if they would benefit from the information gained from the tests. Bailey is the science editor for Reason *magazine.*

As you read, consider the following questions:

1. According to Bailey, people with two copies of the APOE4 gene have how much of a greater risk of getting Alzheimer's disease?

2. What percent of women over sixty-five will get Alzheimer's disease, according to the author?

3. The author points to previous debate about genetic testing for what disease in support of his argument?

"A final lesson from the history of bioethics is the consensus that if you can't offer a patient anything to prevent or to ameliorate a terrible disease, why test for it?," writes University of Alabama at Birmingham bioethicist Greg Pence in a heartfelt op/ed in the *Birmingham News*. Pence is specifically concerned about burgeoning availability of tests for the brain-and-personality-destroying horror that is Alzheimer's disease.

The Development of New Tests for Alzheimer's Disease

Just last week [January 20, 2011,] an expert panel at the Food and Drug Administration recommended that the agency approve a new test developed by Avid Radiopharmaceuticals that can detect the presence in the brain of plaques of the amyloid protein associated with Alzheimer's disease. The test uses a radioactive dye that attaches to amyloid plaques. That dye can then be detected with positron emission tomography (PET) scans.

Other researchers are developing a test that measures amyloid and other protein levels in spinal fluid. They recently reported that the test found the protein signature for Alzheimer's disease in 90 percent of the patients who had already been diagnosed with the disease. In addition, the test found the disease signature in 72 percent of those who have mild cognitive impairment, and in 36 percent of patients who were cognitively normal. Withdrawing spinal fluid is tricky, so researchers at the University of California, San Francisco, are working on a blood test to predict which patients are likely to suffer from Alzheimer's disease.

Most interestingly in the spinal fluid study, many of the cognitively normal subjects with the Alzheimer's disease signature carry a version of the apolipoprotein E (APOE4) gene. People with one copy of the APOE4 gene have a three times greater than average risk of suffering from the disease. Two copies of the gene confer a 12 times greater than average risk. The researchers [Geert De Meyer et al.] noted, "The unexpected presence of the [Alzheimer's disease] signature in more than one-third of cognitively normal subjects suggests that [Alzheimer's disease] pathology is active and detectable earlier than has heretofore been envisioned." In other words, the test can identify people years in advance who are likely to eventually suffer from the disease.

Opposition to Genetic Testing

Several direct-to-consumer gene testing companies now include an APOE gene test. People with the rare APOE2 version seem to be protected against the disease while those with the APOE3 version have an average risk of coming down with it. The lifetime risk of Alzheimer's disease among those who reach the age of 65 is approximately one in five for women and one in 10 among men. Clearly, the direct-to-consumer gene testing companies are ignoring Pence's bioethical "consensus" about offering tests for incurable diseases.

Why are so many bioethicists against such testing? Chiefly, they fear that bad news will provoke anxiety in people whose lives would be forever deformed by dread of impending mental doom. But is that so? A 2009 study found that subjects who were told their APOE gene status did not suffer any greater levels of anxiety than people who did not know what version of the APOE gene they carry. "The disclosure of *APOE* genotyping results to adult children of patients with Alzheimer's disease did not result in significant short-term psychological risks," researchers [Robert C. Green et al.] concluded.

This result has now been bolstered by another study published online on January 12, 2011, in the *New England Journal of Medicine*. Eric Topol, a professor of translational genomics and his colleagues at the Scripps Translational Science Institute in La Jolla, California, recruited 3,600 people to take a genotype screening test from Navigenics. The test looks for gene variants that affect risks for 23 different diseases including breast cancer, colon cancer, heart attack, diabetes, and the APOE gene variants. The researchers then monitored the participants to find out if the genetic risk information increased their anxiety or encouraged them to change their health habits. The researchers reported, "We found no short-term changes in psychological health, diet and exercise behavior, or use of screening tests." The test results triggered no dark existential anxieties; people basically just carried on with their lives.

The Consequences of Genetic Testing

We've experienced this kind of bioethical condescension before. In 1998, a panel of eminent bioethicists convened at Stanford University advised that most women should not take the new test for the BRCA-1 and BRCA-2 breast cancer genes. As Boston University bioethicist George Annas familiarly explained, "Since there is no way to prevent this disease, what good is knowing you will probably get it in the future?" In addition, the bioethicists [B.A. Koenig et al.] worried, "Women who undergo genetic testing may face psychological problems in adjusting to the results, whether positive or negative." Poor dears, they will just be driven to distraction by the newfangled test results. But once again, bioethical fears about the psychological fragility of consumers turned out to be just wrong. A 2008 study found that women four years after taking the BRCA test had suffered no adverse psychological consequences from it.

The Impact of Genetic Testing

In a selected group of subjects who underwent direct-to-consumer genomewide risk profiling with a commercially available test, prospective short-term assessment of those who completed follow-up did not show measurable changes in anxiety level, dietary fat intake, or exercise behavior after genetic testing. We observed no indication of test-related distress in 90.3% of the subjects and no evidence of increased use of screening tests. Generally speaking, our findings support the null hypothesis (that provision of the results of a direct-to-consumer genomic risk test does not affect health-related behavior), but the potential effects on the population at large are still unknown.

Cinnamon S. Bloss, Nicholas J. Shork, and Eric J. Topol,
"Effect of Direct-to-Consumer Genomewide
Profiling to Age Is Disease Risk," New England
Journal of Medicine, *February 10, 2011.*

The National Cancer Institute estimates lifetime risk for breast cancer in women with BRCA-1 or BRCA-2 mutations at about 60 percent and estimates their ovarian cancer risk ranges from 15 percent to 40 percent. Keep in mind that the average lifetime risk for breast cancer is about 12 percent. Fifteen years later, the American Civil Liberties Union (ACLU) is asserting that not only should access to BRCA testing not be restricted, but that it is a woman's right to get tested. "*Individual patients'* rights are violated because gene patents impede access to medical information and care," argues the ACLU in its lawsuit against the Myriad Genetics, the company that has the patent rights to the test. What was once restricted has become a right. In a few more years, the same will become true for Alzheimer's disease testing too.

There are lots of different answers to Pence's question, why test for incurable diseases like Alzheimer's disease? Now that the tests are becoming available, researchers can identify people who are at higher risk of falling ill earlier, and enroll them in studies to uncover how the disease progresses. This will also allow scientists to enroll subjects in clinical trials earlier for new drugs aimed at preventing the disease.

Testing is not just about therapy. People can also use the information to help plan their futures. Perhaps they will drop out of the corporate grind and become Caribbean sailing captains. Or they will arrange their affairs so that they can receive good care when they do fall ill. Of course, some people really may not want to know. In which case, they are perfectly free to not take the tests. The only people who seem especially overwrought and unable to handle the results of genetic testing are bioethicists.

"When it comes to the access issue, to my mind the best model is consumers' right to their own medical records and information."

Direct-to-Consumer Genetic Tests and the Right to Know

Ronni Sandroff

In the following viewpoint, Ronni Sandroff argues that the rise in companies offering direct-to-consumer genetic testing has created controversy. She contends that part of the resistance to such testing is the current lack of medical application for such knowledge. Sandroff concludes that because of this uncertainty, industry claims about genetic tests should be regulated but, nonetheless, consumers should have a right to such knowledge, with or without a medical intermediary. Sandroff is the editorial director of health and family at Consumer Reports.

As you read, consider the following questions:

1. Which government agency, according to Sandroff, discovered contradictory results in a study where it sent out identical genetic samples to several companies?

Ronni Sandroff, "Direct-to-Consumer Genetic Tests and the Right to Know," *Hastings Center Report 40*, no. 5, 2010, pp. 24–25. Copyright © 2010 by The Hastings Center. All rights reserved. Reproduced by permission.

2. The author cites a poll finding what percent of consumers in favor of pharmacies selling home genetic testing kits?

3. What two reasons does Sandroff give in favor of regulating the genetic testing industry?

My daughter recently convinced me to have my first genetic test, after she tested positive for factor V Leiden thrombophilia, a risk factor for blood clotting disorder. My doctor agreed to write an order for the gene test, but she didn't think it would matter much if I tested positive. "After all," she said, "you've lived with it this long."

Waiting for the result, I remember wishing hard that my daughter's mutated gene came from my ex-husband's side of the family, rather than mine. I felt an odd sense of shame at the idea of passing on a bad gene. I was reminded of the old movie about a young murderer called *The Bad Seed*. Bad genes seemed a stain on my family pride.

Dealing with genetic knowledge is new for many of us, although families with devastating hereditary diseases such as cystic fibrosis and Tay-Sachs have dealt with it for decades. In recent years there's been an avalanche of studies identifying the genes shared by people who have various disorders. Often, the genetic tests become available to the public long before this knowledge has been confirmed or proven useful for predictive purposes. For several years it's been possible to order specific tests or analysis of your whole genome by sending a cheek tissue scraping or saliva sample to a lab. For a fee, some companies will also update the analysis of your genome as new knowledge is uncovered. The price of genetic testing has been falling, but recent efforts to bring it to a wider market have met with resistance.

Pathway Genomics Corporation and Walgreens announced in May that they would offer genetic testing collection kits at the drug chain. The Food and Drug Administration took notice. In a May 10th letter, the agency notified Pathway Genomics that its product, "intended to report customary and personal genetic health disposition results for more than 70 health conditions . . . appears to meet the definition of a device as regulated under the Federal Food and Drug and Cosmetic Act," thus requiring FDA approval. The company has delayed plans to market the product. A similar letter was sent to five other direct-to-consumer testing companies in June.

Most telling, on July 22, the Government Accountability Office released a study in which it sent identical DNA samples to four genetic testing firms to test for fifteen common diseases and conditions. Contradictory results abounded. For example, various companies told a forty-eight-year-old male that he had average, below-average, or above-average risk for prostate cancer. These contradictions can be explained, in part, by the fact that companies analyzed different genetic "markers," and that scientists disagree about what these mean in real-life situations. However, in this study the risk predictions often conflicted with the donors' actual illnesses and family medical histories. One company said a donor had below-average risk of atrial fibrillation, when in fact he had had a pacemaker implanted thirteen years earlier to treat the disease. And, in a separate GAO study of marketing practices, two of fifteen genetic testing companies used information from consumers' profiles to recommend that they buy expensive nutritional supplements.

Right to Know (or Not)

Not surprisingly, a poll that came out after the Walgreens incident found that 74 percent of consumers but only 29 percent of doctors thought it was appropriate for pharmacies to sell home genetic testing kits. This can be viewed as doctors claiming the turf for themselves, or as their attempt to protect themselves from patients bearing genome printouts and demanding help to interpret and use the results—help that doctors are not prepared to deliver. It may also be a genuine expression of concern that this information, provided out of context, is too complex for individuals to deal with.

Interestingly, this paternalism has not been applied to paternity testing. For an over-the-counter kit costing about a hundred and fifty dollars and a few cheek swabs, a man can find out if a child is genetically his. Somehow the public has shown itself capable of handling this fraught information, and everyone assumes the person has a right to know. In fact, the right *not* to know has been debated in this area. For example, if an adult child offers to donate a kidney to a father, the genetic tests done to analyze compatibility may, on occasion, show that father and child are not genetically related. Should the doctor inform the family of this result, given that the test was not taken for that purpose? (All transplant centers in Maryland have now adopted policies to cover the potential discovery of paternity surprises as part of the informed consent process.)

Most genetic prediction of disease risk does not, however, have the certainty of paternity testing. It's one thing to identify genetic markers that distinguish people who do and do not have a particular disease (and good scientific studies may differ on which markers are important). But it's quite another to use those markers to make predictions about healthy people. That requires long-term studies to see if those with particular markers actually contract particular diseases—and this knowledge may be decades away.

The Problem with Probability

Two sorry facts about genetic testing are the best arguments for regulating the testing industry—or at least regulating its claims and the accuracy of materials sent with test results. First, test results are difficult to understand, and, second, knowledge is changing with incredible speed, and sometimes even doing an about-face.

Most genetic tests deal in probability, not certainty; because human destiny involves much more than the subtypes of various bits of DNA. Environmental and historical conditions may heavily influence your health and can also affect your genes themselves, activating or deactivating their expression. So if you find out you have several genetic risk factors for heart disease, and you take steps to eat right, exercise, reduce stress, and perhaps take preventive medications, you may very well evade or even deactivate the genetic risk. And that's the promise that sellers of genetic tests dangle before their customers.

But the field is still in its toddlerhood, and today's truth can be tomorrow's mistake. Take the recent announcement that scientists had discovered a set of genes that lead to a one-hundred-year lifespan. The study was no sooner published online in the journal *Science* than there was an outcry of criticism from the scientific community about its methodology and results.

When we're ill, we are forced to rely on the science of the moment. But when it comes to planning our futures, we can choose to wait for more validated information.

Free Trade or Medical Monopoly?

In this era of easy and instant access to the latest medical and scientific information, should the expert professional still be the gatekeeper? Or can regulation effectively ensure that direct-to-consumer genetic tests come with clear, accurate information about their reliability, offer unbiased professional interpretation, and are not used as marketing devices for unproven products?

When it comes to the access issue, to my mind the best model is consumers' right to their own medical records and information. It's not that long ago that medical records were considered the exclusive property of physicians, not patients. It took consumer advocates a great deal of work to establish the individual's right to see and possess his or her own medical records. Today, if your doctor orders a genetic test, you have the right to see the results.

But do we always need the intermediary? The human genome contains much interesting information, only some of which is related to health. In the United Kingdom, genetic record banks have shown that people who share a surname have genetic likenesses; this has enabled some adopted people to locate their family of origin. Some people have even posted their genomes on the Internet or on dating services for all to see, use, and analyze. But others insist on privacy. The Havasupai Indians fought and won the right to get their blood samples back from Arizona State University scientists when they learned their DNA was being studied for ancestry information and conditions besides diabetes—the topic of the study they had consented to.

Even in the medical arena, if my doctor had not agreed to test for factor V Leiden thrombophilia, I would have liked the option of ordering the test myself. I would also hope that the company that sold it to me would provide accurate information about its trustworthiness and easy access to an unbiased professional who could help me interpret the results.

As it turned out, I was not the parent who passed on the mutated gene. But the test result did not give me the emotional lift I had expected. By then, I had done enough research to realize that it was highly unlikely that I had no negative genes, and that not all of my daughter's risk factors could come from my ex-husband. As our chief medical editor at *Consumer Reports* likes to joke: "The only completely healthy person is the one who hasn't been adequately tested."

So I'm not rushing to get my whole genome tested just yet, out of fear of "too much information"—and highly uncertain information at best. But I'm also anxious to retain the right to do so, if ever I feel the need, or even the curiosity.

> "*Fetal gene testing in balloned numbers and scope will disquiet reproductive rights advocates, disability rights advocates, and many others.*"

One Step Closer to Designer Babies: New Noninvasive Prenatal Genetic Testing Could Change Human Pregnancy Forever

Marcy Darnovsky

In the following viewpoint, Marcy Darnovsky argues that advancement in the area of prenatal genetic testing stands to drastically alter pregnancy, parenthood, and society. Darnovsky claims that because noninvasive prenatal diagnosis will be available early in pregnancy, many prospective parents will be faced with the choice of what to do with potentially dubious genetic information. Darnovsky worries that such information may lead to pregnancy terminations for potential disease, disability, and even for traits such as eye color, leading to serious social and moral implications. Darnovsky is the executive director at the Center for Genetics and Society.

As you read, consider the following questions:

1. According to Darnovsky, amniocentesis and chorionic villus sampling—the two methods of prenatal genetic testing available now—carry what risk of miscarriage?

2. The author suggests that which two gene tests for specific illnesses are helpful and important?

3. Darnovsky raises what concern about how noninvasive prenatal diagnosis may impact health insurance coverage?

A new approach to testing the genes of early-stage fetuses could radically alter the experience of pregnancy and parenting. And we'd better start thinking about it now—before hype, fear, and the polarized politics of abortion distort the discussion.

The technique being developed analyzes fetal DNA that is collected from women's blood as early as five weeks into a pregnancy. So-called "noninvasive prenatal diagnosis," or NIPD, may hit the market as a test for Down syndrome later this year. Soon after, refinements are likely that will allow identification of fetal genes at thousands of sites; two different research groups published papers claiming "proof in principle" of this prospect last December.

Because NIPD would be less invasive, less risky, and less expensive than the kinds of fetal gene tests now available, and because it relies on a simple blood draw so early in pregnancy, it is poised to become a prenatal game changer.

The fetal gene tests now offered are far from a walk in the park. For amniocentesis, a long needle is poked through your abdomen and uterus to extract amniotic fluid when you're about 15–20 weeks pregnant. Chorionic villus sampling takes a snip of placental tissue, acquired by snaking a catheter through your vagina and cervix at 10–12 weeks. Both procedures carry a 0.5 percent to 1 percent risk of miscarriage.

By contrast, for NIPD you'd simply give a little extra blood at the lab at your first prenatal checkup. There would be no risk at all to you or the fetus. And you'd get the results before you were visibly pregnant, before you'd told your mother or your friends.

Of the 5 million or so pregnancies in the United States each year, only a few percent involve amniocentesis or chorionic villus sampling. Another few thousand fetal gene tests are done on embryos created with in vitro fertilization.

These numbers are relatively small. Even so, the practice of selecting fetuses and embryos with particular genes elicits concerns about the implications for people living with the very disabilities that are often "deselected," about sex selection, and about parental expectations of a "perfect" child. NIPD could send the yearly number of fetal gene tests skyrocketing into the millions, and the level of concern soaring.

Researchers developing NIPD have already established partnerships with biotech companies eager to commercialize it; San Diego-based Sequenom has announced it will make NIPD for Down syndrome available in the fourth quarter of this year. Detecting hundreds or thousands of genetic variations, as opposed to particular chromosomal configurations, will be more difficult (and, at least initially, far more expensive). But researchers working on NIPD are confident that they'll soon be able to do just that.

In other words, NIPD might soon be able to present you with the kind of genetic information about your five-week-old fetus that you can get today about yourself by sending a couple hundred dollars and a wad of spit to one of the "direct-to-consumer" gene test companies peddling their wares online. In both cases, you'd get a report that claims to predict risk for scores of common diseases and "conditions."

But what do such reports mean? Predictions based on genetic testing are often highly misleading. You may learn from your own gene test, for example, that your risk of some con-

The Disability Rights Critique of Prenatal Testing

The thought of never having a child with a genetic-based condition, such as Down's syndrome, or Tay-Sachs, or sickle-cell anemia, may sound appealing to some at first. But the consequences for those with these conditions; the effect on parents making these decisions; and the impact on clinicians prompting such selection creates a different picture. To begin, the tensions between prenatal diagnostics and disability existed long before the introduction of NIPD [noninvasive prenatal diagnosis]. The so-called "disability rights critique of prenatal testing" involves three major contentions, including: (1) that prenatal diagnosis to detect disabling traits reinforces the medical model that disability is a problem to be solved, and in so doing, overshadows the more important issue of societal discrimination against people with disabilities; (2) supports parental expectations of "perfect" children; and (3) selective abortions based on predicted disability is too often associated with misinformation about living with and raising a child with a disability.... NIPD effectively works to eliminate the "checkpoints" that currently exist with regards to the use of prenatal genetic diagnosis (i.e. cost, associated risks, additional strain and frustration for surgical procedures); and as such, NIPD threatens to exacerbate and make "routine" the issues that disability advocates are most concerned about.

Lori Haymon,
"Non-Invasive Prenatal Genetic Diagnosis (NIPD),"
Council for Responsible Genetics, 2011.
www.councilforresponsiblegenetics.org.

dition is 50 percent higher than average—but how important is that if the average risk is only 1 percent? You may be told that you have a genetic variation associated with some disease—but that result may be based on one or a couple of small studies that have since been found wanting. The results look impressive and objective but for the most part their meaning is dubious and their usefulness scant. In fact, an increasing number of medical and genetic experts, and an FDA advisory panel, agree that when it comes to predicting common diseases, gene tests are a waste of money. Responsible medical practice, in this view, would limit gene tests to those that are clinically meaningful and useful.

Of course, some gene test results are helpful and important: If you're planning children, for example, you may want to know if you're a carrier for a serious single-gene disorder such as Tay-Sachs; if close relatives have had breast cancer, you may want to learn whether you have the mutation that significantly raises your risk of the rare familial form of the cancer.

But even with genetically imposed risks that are well established—for example, the genetic variation linked to early-onset Alzheimer's—there are often few if any preventive measures to take. Fetal gene testing, however, is different. It presents an option: terminating a previously wanted pregnancy.

If sequencing large swaths of fetal genomes becomes common, that's a choice millions might face. But how could pregnant women and their partners possibly interpret the results of tests that claim to predict dozens or hundreds of a future child's traits? How, for example, could they "balance" a 25 percent increase in one risk against a 15 percent decrease in another? What would any of us do with information like this, even—or especially—if we knew it to be dubious and misleading?

And what of the broader social concerns? How many parents would choose to terminate a pregnancy because their child might be born with a disability—even if it was one with which many people are living full and happy lives? Would health insurers encourage such tests, or even require them, in order to avoid the costs of special-needs children?

It could get worse. Would we see parents using prenatal testing to try for a boy who'd play basketball with Dad or a girl eager to go clothes shopping with Mom? Would we begin to see offers—like the one in 2009 by a Los Angeles fertility clinic—to test fetuses for hair color, eye color, and skin tone?

Two close observers of NIPD's development, UC Hastings legal scholar Jaime King and Stanford bioethicist Henry Greely, predict NIPD will soon force us to face the "brave new world" questions that "we have been able until now to ignore." In a January *Nature* article titled "Get Ready for the Flood of Fetal Gene Screening," Greely described the pending situation in appropriately dramatic terms: The "spectre of eugenics will loom over the whole discussion," he noted. And concerns about eugenics "will increase as such testing moves from fatal diseases to less serious medical conditions and then on to nonmedical characteristics."

Though some will object to NIPD largely because it makes greater numbers of abortions likely, its social and moral implications are not well captured by the abortion debate. Fetal gene testing in ballooned numbers and scope will disquiet reproductive rights advocates, disability rights advocates, and many others. Those of us determined to protect abortion rights will need to find ways to prevent frivolous and medically irrelevant genetic testing that could distort our hard-won reproductive freedoms and carry us into the realm of eugenics.

| "*The separability of testing from abortion . . . makes moral regulation of prenatal testing a logistical nightmare.*"

Prenatal Genetic Testing Has Broad Support, Even with Increased Abortion

William Saletan

In the following viewpoint, William Saletan argues that although widespread availability of noninvasive prenatal testing (NIPT) will almost certainly increase the abortion rate, it is politically untenable to oppose such testing. Saletan contends that public support for prenatal testing, coupled with public support for abortion in the first trimester, means support for NIPT is strong. Furthermore, Saletan contends that it is not possible to allow NIPT or abortion only for selective reasons. Saletan covers science, technology, and politics for Slate.

As you read, consider the following questions:

1. According to Saletan, what five formidable interests are lined up in support of noninvasive prenatal testing?

2. The author refers to a *National Journal* poll finding what ratio of Americans in support of insurance coverage for prenatal testing?

3. Saletan cites a Gallup poll that found what percent of Americans support legal abortion in the first trimester?

Today, if you're pregnant with a defective fetus, you won't know about the problem till you're well along. At 10 to 12 weeks, you can get chorionic villus sampling, which involves extracting tissue from the placenta by going through your abdomen or inserting a tube through your cervix. At 15 weeks or so, you can get amniocentesis, which involves sticking a long needle through your belly to draw amniotic fluid. Both tests are uncomfortable, and in one case out of every 100 to 200, they cause a miscarriage.

The Emergence of Noninvasive Prenatal Testing

That's now changing, thanks to noninvasive prenatal testing (NIPT). As Mara Hvistendahl explained recently in *Slate*, companies are developing tests that can estimate the risk of a defective pregnancy from fetal DNA in the mother's own blood, extracted by a regular needle from her arm, like any other blood draw. That means less risk of miscarriage, less stress, less discomfort, less hassle, and lower cost. It also means earlier detection. This week [May 29, 2012], at a conference at Stanford Law School, companies working on the technology said their tests could screen for defects at 10 weeks. But informally, the expected threshold for NIPT is seven to eight weeks, and possibly five.

What's going to happen to prenatal testing in this country when you can get it earlier, cheaper, and more easily? What will happen to the abortion rate and the population of families affected by, say, Down syndrome? Will pro-lifers and disability groups freak out? Will states restrict the new tests?

I don't think so. I've been looking at recent polling data, as well as the science and practice of prenatal testing. The interests lined up behind NIPT are formidable: parents, disease lobbies, biotech and medical companies, insurers, and governments that fund health care. And on the other side, pro-lifers will have a much harder time fighting NIPT than they've had fighting abortion.

How Public Support for NIPT Relates to Abortion

Americans have always expressed more sympathy for aborting defective fetuses than for abortion in general. In recent polls by Gallup and Fox News, narrow majorities supported legal abortion in the case of fatal defect or physical or mental impairment. Pro-lifers hope to prevent this practice from spreading to less dire conditions. Four years ago, the Ethics and Public Policy Center [EPPC] commissioned a poll showing that 57 percent of U.S. adults thought abortion should be allowed if prenatal tests indicated fatal disease, but only 20 percent thought it should be allowed if tests indicated a "serious, non-fatal" condition such as Down syndrome.

The problem for pro-lifers is that prenatal testing doesn't work this way. It combines some issues and separates others in ways that confound moral distinctions. To begin with, there's an obvious medical and business logic to screening for many conditions in a single test. Once you've assembled fetal DNA from fragments in the mother's blood, you might as well check it for Down syndrome as well as cystic fibrosis. So while some people might condone testing for one disease but not the other, it isn't clear how you'd write, pass, or enforce a law to impose that distinction.

Nor is it clear how you'd impose a distinction between one purpose and another. Take sex selection. The EPPC poll, like others, shows overwhelming opposition to permitting abortions of fetuses just because they're female. Yesterday

[May 31, 2012], a majority of the U.S. House of Representatives voted to outlaw such abortions. But doctors test for fetal sex all the time. They do it because some families carry X-linked disorders, which produce disease in boys, since males don't inherit a second X chromosome to counteract the first one. If sex is a medically legitimate trait to test for, how will you police which women can be told they're carrying girls, and which can't? And once they're told, how can you connect that disclosure to their subsequent decisions? It's not like they're all going to announce to an abortion provider that they want the fetus out because it's a girl.

Look closely at the question in the EPPC poll. It doesn't ask whether testing should be allowed for nonfatal conditions. It asks whether abortions should be allowed based on the test results. Why? Because if you don't mention abortion, Americans don't object to the tests. In a 2004 survey by the Genetics and Public Policy Center, 60 percent of respondents approved of prenatal genetic testing for diseases that wouldn't even show up in the fetus till it reached adulthood. Fifty-one percent approved of testing for fetal sex. In every scenario, support for testing fetuses exceeded support for testing pre-implantation embryos. That's a pretty clear sign that the respondents weren't thinking about abortion.

The Political Ramifications of NIPT

The separability of testing from abortion, coupled with the bundling of testable diseases and the ambiguity of how the findings will be applied, makes moral regulation of prenatal testing a logistical nightmare. It puts pro-lifers in the politically untenable position of opposing information and health care, not just abortion.

Look what happened to Rick Santorum two months ago when he criticized prenatal testing as a gateway to abortion. In a poll published by *National Journal*, a 2-to-1 majority of

Public Support for Abortion Due to Genetic Characteristics

New in-utero testing technologies are allowing parents to know in advance some of the genetic characteristics of their developing child fairly soon after conception, such as its sex or if it has any medical conditions or genetic diseases such as Down syndrome. In some cases, parents may choose to terminate or abort a pregnancy after learning the results of these tests. In which, if any, of the following circumstances do you believe parents should be legally allowed to terminate the pregnancy? [These options were read and rotated, and multiple responses were accepted.]

57%	If they discover the child has a fatal disease or condition that would likely result in its death either before or shortly after birth
20%	If they discover the child has a serious, but non-fatal, genetic disease or condition such as Down syndrome
3%	If they discover the sex of the child is not what they wanted— for example, they wanted a boy and the child is a girl
30%	None of the above (volunteered)
1%	Other (volunteered)
3%	Don't know/not sure (volunteered)
*	Refused (volunteered)

TAKEN FROM: Yuval Levin, "Public Opinion and the Embryo Debates," *New Atlantis*, Spring 2008. www.thenewatlantis.com.

Americans—60 to 30 percent—affirmed not just that prenatal testing should be permitted, but that insurers should be required to pay for it. They took this position even after hearing the anti-abortion argument as part of the poll question. And in a brutal exchange on *Face the Nation*, Bob Schieffer demolished Santorum's position. "Senator, do you not want any kind of prenatal testing?" Schieffer asked. "Would we just turn our back on science" and say "it's best not to know about these things ahead of time?" Santorum was forced to cave.

Ugly as that episode was, an attack on NIPT could get uglier. Santorum was challenging amniocentesis, which takes place in the second trimester. NIPT takes place in the first trimester. Morally, this makes NIPT far more palatable, since the fetus is less developed. Politically, it puts pro-lifers in the awkward position of opposing a technology that could replace second-trimester abortions with first-trimester abortions. Last year, Gallup found that while only 24 percent of Americans thought abortion should be legal in the second trimester, 62 percent thought it should be legal in the first trimester. An attack on NIPT would defy this consensus that earlier is better. And it would leave pro-lifers with the task of explaining why women should be consigned to tests that produce a measurable rate of miscarriage.

The pro-abortion rights aspect of the backlash could be more explosive. The new tests aren't just earlier; they're less invasive. Anyone who opposes them has to explain why women should instead have to endure the tubes and needles of amniocentesis or chorionic villus sampling. Remember what happened earlier this year [2012], when the Virginia legislature passed a bill requiring ultrasound before abortions? A firestorm erupted over the prospect that the bill would require transvaginal ultrasound, in which "a probe . . . covered with a condom and a gel" is inserted into the vagina. Pro-lifers looked like they were mandating sexual abuse. The governor had to ask lawmakers to remove transvaginal ultrasound from the bill. I doubt Republicans want to replay that fight in a debate over invasive prenatal testing.

That doesn't mean pro-lifers can't or shouldn't do anything about NIPT. The availability of easier, cheaper, earlier tests will almost certainly increase the abortion rate. Pro-lifers might succeed in regulating counseling or insurance practices so that ambivalent women don't feel pressured to abort. But the best way to separate testing from abortion is to push the technology forward so that we're fixing defective embryos and fetuses, not just discarding them. Who could be against that?

"Abortion, which removes the illness by destroying the one who carries it, is a science-antagonist."

Testing Ourselves: Researchers Simplify Prenatal Genetic Scans

Charles A. Donovan

In the following viewpoint, Charles A. Donovan argues that new technology allowing prenatal genetic testing using noninvasive methods early in pregnancy runs the risk of impeding science and increasing discrimination. Donovan claims that this testing may lead to dangerous eugenics where fetuses with certain diseases are aborted based on bias and the desire to lower costs. Donovan concludes that more laws are needed to protect from the increased abortions that will eliminate all perceived disabilities rather than using science to cure them. Donovan is president of the Susan B. Anthony List Education Fund.

As you read, consider the following questions:

1. According to Donovan, new prenatal genetic testing using maternal blood and paternal saliva can identify approximately how many diseases?

2. What percent of fetuses with Down syndrome are aborted, according to the author?

3. What piece of legislation does the author identify as beneficial in counteracting discrimination against individuals and families?

Consider for a moment any random collection of 20 people of your acquaintance. Include your banker. The captain of your high-school football team. The mentally ill veteran on the street corner who accepts a quarter from you twice a week. The perpetually smiling vendor in a wheelchair at the Metro stop who sells you candy for a dollar. The lawyer representing the automobile-insurance company suing you for damages in a recent accident. The student activist who thrust a flyer into your hand on Earth Day.

Now rank these people in order of their inherent superiority and contribution to humanity. If it seems an impossible task not delegated to the human mind or human hands, it is becoming ever clearer that the temptation to rank, to score, and to impose cut-offs on entry into the human community is mounting. This week [June 2012] researchers at the University of Washington have published results in the journal *Science Translational Medicine* demonstrating the ability to identify inherited genetic diseases and new mutations in the unborn using only maternal blood and paternal saliva.

The new testing capacity is extraordinarily expensive—$20,000 to $50,000 per sequencing—but, like the price of computer memory—it is likely to drop rapidly. According to some commentators, commercially feasible testing could be affordable in three to five years. We are not quite at the point where expectant parents will stroll up to a testing booth seeking a DNA scan like Uma Thurman's character in *Gattaca*, but we are getting closer.

The speed with which this testing advances will, ironically, draw upon the fact that it is initially beneficial to at least some of the developing babies that will be tested. Today's most prevalent methods for genetic testing of the unborn, e.g., chorionic villus sampling (CVS), are by an invasive method with risk of fetal loss. Movement to a test that involves taking parental blood and saliva samples that look for and compare that DNA with fetal DNA fragments in the mother's blood will initially spare the lives of some children not subjected to CVS or amniocentesis. But given the thoroughness of the sequencing (allowing the identification of some 3,000 genetic diseases that affect roughly 1 percent of pregnancies), the new process may expose others, perhaps many more, to abortion.

The presence or mere propensity for disease, of course, will not be the only information rendered available by such testing. Sex, eye and hair color, athletic ability, and countless other characteristics will be, to some degree, ascertainable through such means. In the 20th century the movements for negative and positive eugenics operated on the basis of generalized and typically false criteria—bias and ignorance, in short; the science of genome sequencing is more exact, and therefore more exploitable by societal forces that urge the early elimination of those with certain diseases as a cost-saving alternative to researching and curing diseases themselves.

The recent history of Down-syndrome research and testing is instructive. While estimates vary, all are agreed that the vast majority of children diagnosed prenatally with this illness in the United States are aborted—perhaps 90 percent or more. At the same time, and with much less fanfare, continuing (but radically underfunded) research and the devotion of parents who have borne Down's children and raised them with love, have resulted in longer lifespans and expansion of the horizons of hope for these men and women. In 2011, as the Jerome LeJeune Foundation reports, the first clinical trial of a therapeutic modality for Trisomy 21 was launched. Already there are five trials underway. We need many more.

The amassing of knowledge about the genome and its operations is irresistible and ultimately, in an ethically wise universe, of immense potential benefit. Science is not the problem. Ironically, abortion, which removes the illness by destroying the one who carries it, is a science-antagonist. All diseases could be handled this way, and from such measures we learn next to nothing. Real science is done when illness is combated, resisted, and overcome.

It is unfortunate that gains in knowledge are coming in an era where disrespect for human life is rampant and fears about growing expenditures for health care are rising. But it is fortunate in turn that we are more alert to the dangers of using genetic information against individuals. The Genetic Information Nondiscrimination Act of 2008, championed by then-senators Sam Brownback and the late Ted Kennedy, erected the first bulwark against the kind of raw cost-benefit calculus and discrimination that would have inevitably occurred against individuals and families in this context.

Such laws are a start, and perhaps they will, with greater awareness, assist in ameliorating the kind of internalized eugenics that tempts us to believe that only a life without disability is worth living. Or even that all of us are not, in some manner, disabled.

Periodical and Internet Sources Bibliography

The following articles have been selected to supplement the diverse views presented in this chapter.

Ronald Bailey	"I'll Show You My Genome. Will You Show Me Yours?," *Reason*, January 2011.
Shannon Brownlee	"Google's Guinea Pigs," *Mother Jones*, November–December 2009.
Lori Haymon	"Non-Invasive Prenatal Genetic Diagnosis (NIPD)," Council for Responsible Genetics, 2011. www.councilforresponsiblegenetics.org.
Matthew Hennessey	"Down Syndrome and the Purpose of Prenatal Testing," *First Things*, August 1, 2011. www.firstthings.com.
Mara Hvistendahl	"Will *Gattaca* Come True?," *Slate*, April 27, 2012. www.slate.com.
Jaime S. King	"And Genetic Testing for All . . . The Coming Revolution in Non-Invasive Prenatal Genetic Testing," *Rutgers Law Journal*, 2011.
Ricki Lewis	"Prenatal Genetic Testing: When Is It 'Toxic Knowledge?'," *DNA Science Blog*, October 18, 2012. www.blogs.plos.org/dnascience.
Christopher Mims	"Tell Me What's in My Genome!," *Slate*, November 25, 2011. www.slate.com.
Bonnie Rochman	"Why Cheaper Genetic Testing Could Cost Us a Fortune," *Time*, October 26, 2012.
David Shenk	"The Limits of Genetic Testing," *Atlantic*, April 3, 2012. www.theatlantic.com.
Harriet A. Washington	"Do You Really Want to Know Your Baby's Genetics?," *New Scientist*, September 16, 2012.

For Further Discussion

Chapter 1

1. It is noted in both the viewpoint of Trudie Lang and Sisira Siribaddana and the viewpoint of Donald L. Barlett and James B. Steele that there has been a growth in clinical trials overseas. In what way, however, do the viewpoints diverge in commenting on the regulations governing overseas clinical trials?

2. Drawing upon the viewpoints of the National Institutes of Health and Carl Elliott, give two reasons in favor of paying healthy volunteers in clinical trials and two reasons against such payment. Which position do you think is the strongest?

Chapter 2

1. The Presidential Commission for the Study of Bioethical Issues suggests areas for improvement in the federal oversight of biomedical research. Do you think its suggestions would satisfy the concerns raised by Jeanne Lenzer and Shannon Brownlee? Why or why not?

2. Name three points of disagreement on the issue of animal experimentation between People for the Ethical Treatment of Animals (PETA) and Americans for Medical Progress. Which organization has the stronger argument, in your view?

Chapter 3

1. Considering the viewpoints in this chapter by John Crewdson, the National Cancer Institute, T.E. Holt, and Nick Tate, name two similarities in the arguments supporting routine mammograms and prostate-specific antigen tests and two similarities in the arguments against.

2. After reading the viewpoints in this chapter, do you believe that government regulations play a positive role in debates about medical diagnostic tests? Why or why not? Explain using specific examples from the viewpoints.

Chapter 4

1. Considering the arguments raised in the viewpoints of Greg Pence, Ronald Bailey, and Ronni Sandroff, what is the strongest argument in favor of allowing consumers access to genetic testing? What is the strongest argument against this? How might one argue that some tests should be allowed but others disallowed?

2. What fact about the relationship between increased prenatal genetic testing and abortion do Marcy Darnovsky, William Saletan, and Charles A. Donovan agree upon? For those who are against abortion, should that impact their support for prenatal genetic testing? Why or why not?

Organizations to Contact

The editors have compiled the following list of organizations concerned with the issues debated in this book. The descriptions are derived from materials provided by the organizations. All have publications or information available for interested readers. The list was compiled on the date of publication of the present volume; names, addresses, phone and fax numbers, and e-mail and Internet addresses may change. Be aware that many organizations take several weeks or longer to respond to inquiries, so allow as much time as possible.

American Medical Association (AMA)
515 N. State Street, Chicago, IL   60654
(800) 621-8335
website: www.ama-assn.org

The American Medical Association is a professional association of physicians and medical students. The AMA works to promote scientific advancement, improve public health, and invest in the doctor and patient relationship. The AMA provides information on its website about a variety of medical tests, including its recommendations regarding testing.

American Society of Law, Medicine, and Ethics (ASLME)
765 Commonwealth Ave., Suite 1634, Boston, MA   02215
(617) 262-4990 • fax: (617) 437-7596
email: info@aslme.org
website: www.aslme.org

The American Society of Law, Medicine, and Ethics is a non-profit educational organization focused on the intersection of law, medicine, and ethics. ASLME aims to provide a forum to exchange ideas in order to protect public health, reduce health disparities, promote quality of care, and facilitate dialogue on emerging science. ASMLE publishes two journals: *Journal of Law, Medicine and Ethics* and *American Journal of Law and Medicine*.

Center for Bioethics and Human Dignity (CBHD)
Trinity International University, 2065 Half Day Road
Deerfield, IL 60015
(847) 317-8180 • fax: (847) 317-8101
email: info@cbhd.org
website: www.cbhd.org

The Center for Bioethics and Human Dignity aims to explore the nexus of biomedicine, biotechnology, and humanity. Within a Judeo-Christian Hippocratic framework, CBHD engages in research, theological and conceptual analysis, charitable critique, and teaching. Among the information available on its website are reports and podcasts, including the podcast "Health Research for Developing Countries: Reason and Emotion in Bioethics."

Center for Genetics and Society (CGS)
1936 University Ave., Suite 350, Berkeley, CA 94704
(510) 625-0819 • fax: (510) 665-8760
email: info@geneticsandsociety.org
website: www.geneticsandsociety.org

The Center for Genetics and Society is a nonprofit information and public affairs organization working to encourage responsible use and effective societal governance of the new human genetic and reproductive technologies. CGS works with scientists, health professionals, and civil society leaders to oppose applications of new human genetic and reproductive technologies that objectify and commodify human life and threaten to divide human society. CGS publishes articles on its website, including "New Business Plans for the Direct-to-Consumer Gene Testing Industry?"

Council for Responsible Genetics (CRG)
5 Upland Road, Suite 3, Cambridge, MA 02140
(617) 868-0870 • fax: (617) 491-5344
email: crg@gene-watch.org
website: www.councilforresponsiblegenetics.org

The Council for Responsible Genetics is a nonprofit organization dedicated to fostering public debate about the social, ethical, and environmental implications of genetic technologies. CRG works through the media and concerned citizens to distribute information and represent the public interest on emerging issues in biotechnology. CRG publishes *GeneWatch*, a magazine dedicated to monitoring biotechnology's social, ethical, and environmental consequences.

Ethics and Public Policy Center (EPPC)
1730 M Street NW, Suite 910, Washington, DC   20036
(202) 682-1200 • fax: (202) 408-0632
website: www.eppc.org

The Ethics and Public Policy Center is dedicated to applying the Judeo-Christian moral tradition to critical issues of public policy. Through its core programs, such as Bioethics and American Democracy, EPPC and its scholars work to influence policy makers and transform the culture through the world of ideas. EPPC publishes the *New Atlantis*, a quarterly journal about technology with an emphasis on bioethics.

Genetics and Public Policy Center
Johns Hopkins University, Berman Institute of Bioethics
Washington, DC   20036
(202) 663-5971 • fax: (202) 663-5992
email: gppcnews@jhu.edu
website: www.dnapolicy.org

The Genetics and Public Policy Center works to help policy makers, the press, and the public understand the challenges and opportunities of genetic medicine. The Genetics and Public Policy Center conducts legal research and policy analysis, performs policy-relevant social science research, and crafts policy recommendations. Available on the center's website are numerous reports and testimony transcripts, including the report "Tables of Direct-to-Consumer Genetic Testing Companies and Conditions Tested."

Hastings Center
21 Malcolm Gordon Road, Garrison, NY   10524-4125
(845) 424-4040 • fax: (845) 424-4545
email: mail@thehastingscenter.org
website: www.thehastingscenter.org

The Hastings Center is a nonprofit bioethics research institute that works to address fundamental ethical issues in the areas of health, medicine, and the environment as they affect individuals, communities, and societies. The Hastings Center conducts research and education and collaborates with policy makers to identify and analyze the ethical dimensions of their work. The Hastings Center publishes two periodicals: *Hastings Center Report* and *IRB: Ethics and Human Research.*

National Human Genome Research Institute (NHGRI)
National Institutes of Health, Bethesda, MD   20892-2152
(301) 402-0911 • fax: (301) 402-2218
website: www.genome.gov

The National Human Genome Research Institute led the National Institutes of Health's contribution to the International Human Genome Project, which had as its primary goal the sequencing of the human genome. NHGRI supports the development of resources and technology that will accelerate genome research and its application to human health. NHGRI has many educational tools available on its website, including lectures and handouts from its Current Topics in Genome Analysis lecture series.

National Institutes of Health (NIH)
9000 Rockville Pike, Bethesda, MD   20892
(301) 496-4000
email: nihinfo@od.nih.gov
website: www.nih.gov

The National Institutes of Health is part of the US Department of Health and Human Services, the nation's medical research agency. NIH is the largest source of funding for medical research in the world, with much of the funding going to universities and research institutions for medical testing on animals and humans. NIH maintains a searchable registry of clinical trials at ClinicalTrials.gov.

US Food and Drug Administration (FDA)
10903 New Hampshire Ave., Silver Spring, MD   20993
(888) 463-6332
website: www.fda.gov

The Food and Drug Administration is an agency within the US Department of Health and Human Services. The FDA is responsible for protecting public health by assuring food and drug safety. The FDA's website contains a variety of information on FDA regulation of drug safety, including information about the development and approval process overseen by the FDA's Center for Drug Evaluation and Research.

Bibliography of Books

Roberto Abadie — *The Professional Guinea Pig: Big Pharma and the Risky World of Human Subjects.* Durham, NC: Duke University Press, 2010.

Michael Arribas-Ayllon, Srikant Sarangi, and Angus Clarke — *Genetic Testing: Accounts of Autonomy, Responsibility, and Blame.* New York: Routledge, 2011.

Mary Ann Baily and Thomas H. Murray, eds. — *Ethics and Newborn Genetic Screening: New Technologies, New Challenges.* Baltimore: John Hopkins University Press, 2009.

Dena S. Davis — *Genetic Dilemmas: Reproductive Technology, Parental Choices, and Children's Futures.* New York: Oxford University Press, 2010.

James M. DuBois — *Ethics in Mental Health Research: Principles, Guidance, and Cases.* New York: Oxford University Press, 2008.

Carl Elliott — *White Coat, Black Hat: Adventures on the Dark Side of Medicine.* Boston: Beacon Press, 2010.

Jill A. Fisher — *Medical Research for Hire: The Political Economy of Pharmaceutical Clinical Trials.* New Brunswick, NJ: Rutgers University Press, 2009.

Jeremy R. Garrett, ed. — *The Ethics of Animal Research: Exploring the Controversy.* Cambridge, MA: MIT Press, 2012.

P. Wenzel Geissler and Catherine Molyneux, eds. — *Evidence, Ethos and Experiment: The Anthropology and History of Medical Research in Africa.* New York: Berghahn Books, 2011.

Masha Gessen — *Blood Matters: From Inherited Illness to Designer Babies, How the World and I Found Ourselves in the Future of the Gene.* New York: Houghton Mifflin Harcourt, 2009.

John Harris — *Enhancing Evolution: The Ethical Case for Making Better People.* Princeton, NJ: Princeton University Press, 2010.

Jennifer Hawkins and Ezekiel Emanuel — *Exploitation and Developing Countries: The Ethics of Clinical Research.* Princeton, NJ: Princeton University Press, 2008.

Matti Häyry — *Rationality and the Genetic Challenge: Making People Better?* New York: Cambridge University Press, 2010.

A.J. Jacobs — *The Guinea Pig Diaries: My Life as an Experiment.* New York: Simon & Schuster, 2009.

Sheila Jasanoff, ed. — *Reframing Rights: Bioconstitutionalism in the Genetic Age.* Cambridge, MA: MIT Press, 2011.

Robert Klizman — *Am I My Genes? Confronting Fate and Family Secrets in the Age of Genetic Testing.* New York: Oxford University Press, 2012.

Adriana Petryna — *When Experiments Travel: Clinical Trials and the Global Search for Human Subjects.* Princeton, NJ: Princeton University Press, 2009.

Aviad E. Raz — *Community Genetics and Genetic Alliances: Eugenics, Carrier Testing, and Networks of Risk.* New York: Routledge, 2010.

Susan Reverby — *Examining Tuskegee: The Infamous Syphilis Study and Its Legacy.* Chapel Hill, NC: University of North Carolina Press, 2009.

Adil E. Shamoo and David B. Resnik — *Responsible Conduct of Research.* New York: Oxford University Press, 2009.

Frida Simonstein, ed. — *Reprogen-ethics and the Future of Gender.* New York: Springer, 2009.

Terry L. Smith — *Modern Genetic Science: New Technology, New Decisions.* New York: Rosen, 2009.

Rickie Solinger — *Reproductive Politics: What Everyone Needs to Know.* New York: Oxford University Press, 2013.

Stefan Timmermans and Mara Buchbinder — *Saving Babies?: The Consequences of Newborn Genetic Screening.* Chicago: University of Chicago Press, 2013.

Carlos Valverde, ed. — *Genetic Screening of Newborns: An Ethical Inquiry.* New York: Nova Science Publishers, 2010.

H. Gilbert Welch, Lisa M. Schwartz, and Steven Woloshin — *Overdiagnosed: Making People Sick in the Pursuit of Health.* Boston: Beacon Press, 2011.

David S. Wendler — *The Ethics of Pediatric Research.* New York: Oxford University Press, 2010.

Index

A

Abbott Laboratories, 85–87

Abortions
controversy over, 187
genetic testing concerns and, 194–198, 196*t*
opposition to, 166
selective abortions, 191

Accreditation of Laboratory Animal Care International (AAALAC), 113

Ad libitum feeding, 67–68

Affordable Care Act, 160, 162

Alzheimer's disease
apolipoprotein E (APOE4) gene, 169, 176, 190
new tests for, 175–176, 178–179
testing risks, 170–172

American Board of Internal Medicine Foundation, 120

American Cancer Society (ACS), 108, 124–125

American Civil Liberties Union (ACLU), 178

American College of Cardiology, 145

American College of Physicians, 120

American College of Radiology (ACR), 124, 136

American Urological Association, 138

American Veterinary Medical Association (AVMA) Guidelines on Euthanasia, 114

Americans for Medical Progress, 111–117

Amniocentesis testing, 188, 193, 197, 201

Animal testing
breeding animals for, 116–117
caring for animals, 112–113
citing in biomedical research papers, 69
control animals, 66–68
controversy over, 15
as cruel and unnecessary, 104–110
fight over, 110
human health improvements and, 105–107
as humane and necessary, 111–117
lack of regulation, 108–109
methods used for, 114
moral obligations over, 115–116
overview, 112, 114–115
public funding of, 108
See also Rodents in testing

Animal Welfare Act (AWA), 79, 109, 113

Annals of Internal Medicine (journal), 107

Annas, George, 177

Antibiotics overuse, 155

Apolipoprotein E (APOE4) gene, 169, 176

Arizona State University, 185

Aventis Pharmaceuticals (Sanofi-Aventis), 35

B

C

D

N

CPSIA information can be obtained
at www.ICGtesting.com
Printed in the USA
FFOW05n1825270214